Family, [Friends,] and War Heroes

Reflections From World War II

*To Vic
Thank you for your
service to our great country.
Best wishes & God bless.
Darrell R. Fleming
Dec. 4, 2010*

Darrell R. Fleming

ISBN: 978-1-891029-52-3

Copyright 2005 by Darrell R. Fleming. All rights reserved. The information contained within the covers of this book may not be reproduced without the expressed written consent of Darrell R. Fleming.

Cover Illustration:
A Painting of The USS HOPPING, DE 155/APD 51
by Lt. Laverne Bordwell, Chief Engineering Officer

To Order:
www. AppalachianAGA.com
www.Amazon.com

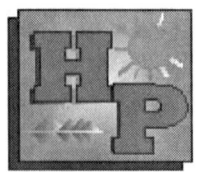

HENDERSON PUBLISHING
811 Eva's Walk, Pounding Mill, VA 24637

Reviews

This book documents some of the important events of World War II which were experienced by the author's family, especially his father who served as a sailor aboard the USS HOPPING. Fleming's in-depth research of this ship and other men aboard the Hopping, along with his personal notes throughout, make this a very interesting and accurate account of an important period of our country's history. A number of dramatic personal stories of these sailor's experiences make it even more compelling. I believe this book would make a solid contribution to our understanding of the American people and our men in service during this period of our history.

-Helen E. Grenga, Ph. D.

Helen E. Grenga, Ph. D., author, **Movies on the Fantail,** *(Yeoman Press, 2001); Associate Vice President and Dean of Graduate Studies and Research, Georgia Tech (retired).*

*****

Commenced reading the book, read until 01:00 AM, went to bed and had a difficult time falling asleep as so many instances experienced by the men aboard this ship just kept coming to mind. The old saying, "Been there.....Done that.", was so very real. It is an interesting story of the impact World War II had on this nation, the family of Truman and Violet Fleming as well as the officers and men who served aboard a destroyer escort. The use of personal and family information as well as the ship's log with dates, events and actual stories about the men who were there is commendable and provides the continuity which kept the entire story flowing from page to page.

-Thomas L. Kidd

Thomas L. Kidd, served as a radarman and Petty Officer aboard the USS K. M. WILLETT, DE 354 from 1944 to 1946; Past President, Destroyer Escort Sailors Association (DESA); Manager, General Electric Metal Fabrication, Drive Systems Department (retired).

Dedication

In memory of my father and mother who guided me into adulthood with their values, morals and examples that are with me today.

To my brothers, Charles, Bill and Buford and my sisters, Anna, Fern and Charlene and their spouses who are a real joy to be with and are my best friends.

To my dear wife, Kathy, who has been my faithful companion and closest friend for fifty-two wonderful years.

To my children, Kent and Tamara, and their spouses, Judy and Ian, for their love, friendship, respect and encouragement. May they know from this, some of the sacrifices their grandparents made so they could enjoy a better life.

To my grandson, Andrew James Sole, who has brought untold joy to me in just four years. From this account, may he come to a better understanding of his family's heritage and the sacrifices that were made decades ago so he could have a life of freedom. It is my hope and prayer that he will take advantage of his gifts and talents and apply them to make his world a better place for all mankind.

And to the men who served on the USS HOPPING, DE 155/APD 51. They served honorably and responsibly and carried out every mission with dedication to a just cause. All contributed their part to achieve victory for the benefit of all mankind. May they always receive the respect and gratitude they deserve from a grateful nation.

Acknowledgements

A special thanks to my wife, Kathy, who spent many hours alone while I was doing research and writing and who traveled many miles with me gathering information and attending ships reunions.

To my daughter, Tamara C. Sole, who provided her computer expertise in preparation of the manuscript and who carefully read it and made many helpful suggestions, my special thanks for her patience, understanding and assistance. There were times I felt I could not have completed it without her help.

I am grateful to those who read the manuscript: Dr. Helen E. Grenga, Thomas L. Kidd, and William Wenzel. Their suggestions and encouragements gave my questioning soul the lift needed to complete the project.

My deepest gratitude and appreciation is extended to the following men who served on the USS HOPPING, DE 155/APD 51: Robert M. "Shorty" Miller, who so willingly shared his storehouse of knowledge, information and pictures; Willis "Bill" Dailey, who shared his letters written to his family while aboard the Hopping; and William H. Wenzel who gave permission to use his writings which added immensely to this project and who read the manuscript and encouraged me to complete it. And to all other Hopping shipmates with whom I spoke by telephone or met personally who contributed their comments, explanations, encouragement and friendship, I will be eternally grateful.

Thanks to Robert O. "Rob" Davidson, for his contributions in presenting a more complete account of the events surrounding the USS DONNELL, DE 56 than I could have assembled.

To Jim Klepper, CEO, Tri-State Chapter of the Destroyer Escort Sailors Association, I owe a debt of gratitude for his assistance and constant encouragement throughout the entire project.

PHOTOGRAPHIC ACKNOWLEDGMENTS

The photographs, sketches, poems, etc. were provided by those listed on the referenced pages. Photographs and items not otherwise acknowledged are from my mother's collection.

Robert O. "Rob" Davidson: pp. 45 (both), 46, 48, 50, 58, 59 (all), 62(both)

James Klepper: p. 12 (Taken from a Destroyer Escort Sailors Association, Inc. newspaper article, date unknown)

Bryan McLaughlin: pp. 73 (bottom), 74 (bottom)

Robert M. "Shorty" Miller: pp. 16 (both), 17, 18, 19, 20, 23, 63, 83, 84 (both), 86, 89, 97, 99, 128, 132, 133

Hy Sheiner: pp. 100 (both), 117, 126, 139, 140 (both), 141, 142 (both), 143 (both)

Howard M. "Howie" Tiedemann: p. 61 (both)

William Wenzel: pp. 13, 137

Contents

		Page
Reviews		*i*
Dedication		*ii*
Acknowledgements		*iii*
Photographic Acknowledgements		*iv*
About the Author		*vii*
William Truman Fleming S 1/C		*viii*

Chapter One	*The Beginning Of The Diary*	*1*
Chapter Two	*A Hurried "Boot Camp"*	*7*
Chapter Three	*Delayed Assignment*	*15*
Chapter Four	*On Board And Training Exercises*	*25*
Chapter Five	*Forming A Convoy And Escort Duty*	*33*
Chapter Six	*Imagine Seeing You Here*	*39*
Chapter Seven	*Rediscovery Of The Diary And More from A Survivor of the USS DONNELL*	*55*
Chapter Eight	*"Make The Best Out Of Life You Can"*	*65*
Chapter Nine	*Keeping Up The Home Front*	*81*
Chapter Ten	*Converting The Hopping To An APD And Off To The Pacific*	*95*
Chapter Eleven	*Dad, The Hopping And The Battle Of Okinawa*	*113*
Chapter Twelve	*The USS HOPPING, APD 51 From Okinawa To Tokyo Bay And Home*	*139*
Chapter Thirteen	*Dad's Homecoming, Successes And Trials*	*151*
Chapter Fourteen	*Friends And War Heroes*	*161*

About the Author

Darrell R. Fleming

Darrell R. Fleming grew up in Clintwood, Dickenson County, Virginia. He graduated from Union College with majors in English and History/Political Science and from The University of Virginia with a Master of Education degree.

After serving two years in the United States Army as a cryptographer with the Seventh Army in Germany, he began teaching in Fairfax County Public Schools, Fairfax, Virginia. He taught nine years at the secondary level and then became an administrator at the high school level before moving to Coordinator of Human Resources for Fairfax County Schools, retiring in 1988.

He now lives with his wife, Kathy, in Blountville, Tennessee and enjoys reading, traveling, golfing and fishing.

William Truman Fleming, S 1/C

Chapter One

The Beginning of the Diary

World War II, 1938-1945, was truly a world at war! Devastation spread from the serene green pastures of England and Ireland, to the industrial cities of Europe, to the majestic mountains of Austria and northern Italy, to the deserts of Africa, to the crowded cities of central and eastern Asia, to the beautiful, peaceful islands of the Pacific including "down under" Australia and New Zealand, to the entire western hemisphere with its vast resources and energy. All countries felt the impact and, if they were spared from the actual war machinery which killed an estimated sixty million people worldwide, they were most definitely affected indirectly through economic and social conditions beyond their control. It seemed, even to the distant observer, that the world was either under fire, on fire or about to be set afire. Such were the dark, dim and dreary days of late 1943 when the Axis powers had marched, cruised and flown around the entire globe to wreak havoc unmercifully on the innocent as well as their targeted populations when this account begins to tell a story of how the war dramatically impacted our family's life for at least two generations.

As a lad of 9 ½ years in late December, 1943, I had been made aware of the menace posed by these evil powers by my father, mother, maternal grandfather and, of course, the radio news media as reported nightly by Gabriel Heater who was a regular listening diet in our home. Further awareness was made clear by the families in our small mountainous community who were so dramatically affected by their youth leaving "to do my part", by the wounded returning home, by the "missing in action" notices or the "killed in action" telegrams which caused untold grief and pain to the recipients. Not to mention the loneliness, fear, discomfort, physical pain and ultimate sacrifice suffered by the men and women who so dutifully served their country. These were tough times that were experienced to different degrees by every person living in the "civilized" world.

My parents, William Truman Fleming and Violet Esther Crabtree Fleming were born in 1913 and 1911 respectfully, in Clintwood, Dickenson County, Virginia which is located in a remote, mountainous section of the southwestern part of the state. Their forefathers had followed Daniel Boone's westward expansion movement to settle in this area because they were seeking their independence from tyranny and oppression. But, as "progress" continued its steady march through the history of mankind, this great war reached our home in a most personal and powerful way.

My parents were married on June 23, 1930 at the very height of the Great Depression. They began their lives together by moving to a small farm owned by my paternal grandparents and immediately began a family in a small two bedroom house with no indoor plumbing, a coal burning cook stove and two open fire places to provide heat. Dad worked in the local industry at the time which was cutting virgin timber for a large lumber company. In addition, he continued to maintain the small farm of about 64 acres, growing hay and corn and raising several hogs and about 200 chickens.

Then he moved to the budding coal mining industry which was just beginning to develop and provide employment for local residents. This employment led him to a large coal company operating in Kentucky by the name of Consolidated Coal Company which was headquartered in Pittsburgh, Pennsylvania. He worked in less than desirable conditions for several years even though the leader of the United Mine Workers of America, President John L. Lewis, worked tirelessly to improve working conditions. During this time, we hardly saw him because he worked such long hours and had to travel hours by car to and from work. In fact, when we did see him he was covered with black coal dust and had that certain damp, pungent smell that only a coal miner or his family could recognize.

Thus began their life together and for the next ten years their family grew to six active and healthy children in a closely knitted family circle.

Truman and Violet Fleming, early 1930's

By the late 1930's and early 1940's the country was beginning to recover from the economic depression and things were improving for their young, growing family until, "... the day that shall live in infamy", December 7, 1941! The United States now being fully engaged in warfare with the Allied Forces against the Axis, their lives changed quickly and dramatically again.

The war effort on the home front in 1942 was moving at a vastly accelerated pace when Dad decided to relocate the family to Radford, Virginia where he worked in the Hercules Powder Plant which produced ammunition to support the war. This lasted about one year because he was always involved in politics back home and with the upcoming election of 1943 he decided to return to Clintwood to participate in electing candidates for his party. The election was hotly contested by the candidates and their supporters and apparently Dad's candidate was elected because he was appointed Deputy Commissioner of Revenue for Dickenson County to take office in January, 1944.

Notice of Classification, front

Notice of Classification, back

    The Selective Service Board or Draft Board, as they were locally known, had a majority membership of the opposing political persuasion; therefore, Dad was convinced that they wanted to "get even" for his political activism during the recent election. So, on December 27, 1943 he received his draft notice even though he was just three months from his thirty first birthday of March 23, 1913 and had a wife and six children at home!

Recently I was able to confirm with the Selective Service Board in Washington, DC that in October, 1943, the Selective Service Act was repealed and signed by President Roosevelt to include men 18 to 38 years old with as many as 10 children and 3,323,970 men were drafted into service that year. In addition, I was informed that draftees who were 30

> **App. not Req.**
>
> **Prepare in Duplicate**
>
> Local Board No. 1
> Dickenson County   049
> **JAN 14 1944**   001
> Court House
> Clintwood, Va.
> (LOCAL BOARD DATE STAMP WITH CODE)
>
> January 14, 1944
> (Date of mailing)
>
> **ORDER TO REPORT FOR INDUCTION**
>
> The President of the United States,
>
> To William   Truman   Fleming
> (First name)   (Middle name)   (Last name)
>
> Order No. 479
>
> **GREETING:**
>
> Having submitted yourself to a local board composed of your neighbors for the purpose of determining your availability for training and service in the land or naval forces of the United States, you are hereby notified that you have now been selected for training and service therein.
>
> You will, therefore, report to the local board named above at Court House, Clintwood, Virginia
> (Place of reporting)
>
> at 7:00 a. m., on the 29th day of January, 19 44
>
> This local board will furnish transportation to an induction station. You will there be examined, and, if accepted for training and service, you will then be inducted into the land or naval forces.
> Persons reporting to the induction station in some instances may be rejected for physical or other reasons. It is well to keep this in mind in arranging your affairs, to prevent any undue hardship if you are rejected at the induction station. If you are employed, you should advise your employer of this notice and of the possibility that you may not be accepted at the induction station. Your employer can then be prepared to replace you if you are accepted, or to continue your employment if you are rejected.
> Willful failure to report promptly to this local board at the hour and on the day named in this notice is a violation of the Selective Training and Service Act of 1940, as amended, and subjects the violator to fine and imprisonment.
> If you are so far removed from your own local board that reporting in compliance with this order will be a serious hardship and you desire to report to a local board in the area of which you are now located, go immediately to that local board and make written request for transfer of your delivery for induction, taking this order with you.
>
> W. H. Smith
> Member or clerk of the local board.
>
> D. S. S. Form 150
> (Revised 1-15-48)

Induction Notice

years and older and had more than four children were usually placed in non-combat duty and most likely in stateside stations. This, however, was not to be Dad's situation.

    Even at my young age, I can recall his coming home from work that December day and joyfully announcing that he had been drafted and would gladly serve his country. One of my brothers remembered that he and my other brother were at the barn milking the cows and taking care of the horses when Dad came to them and told them that he had been drafted and outlined their responsibilities to carry on the duties of the small farm and help mother while he was away.

    His actions of so willingly accepting the draft to serve his country in a time of need left a lasting impression on me and, apparently, on my brothers because three of us voluntarily served our country in the navy, army and air force. The other brother was unable to serve because of an accident and impairment to his leg or I'm sure he would have gladly served also.

    Dad's military record shows that he was inducted on January 29, 1944, Serial Number 935 28 93, at Abingdon, Virginia and enlisted in the U. S. Navy as "A. S. SV6 USNR". He was given orders to report for basic training at Bainbridge, Maryland on February 5, 1944.

    Mother somehow came in possession of a Hartford Fire Insurance Company, 1944 Year Book, from the Clintwood Insurance Agency. It probably was given to her by the owner of the Clintwood Insurance Agency, Mr. F. C. Hillman, from whom they purchased their insurance. In this Year Book the diary was begun by Mother with the following entry:

Monday, January 17, 1944 "Sure hope to read this some day when you return. Love, Violet."

    To which Dad belatedly responded, "I hope to read it too. W.T.F. 4-6-44.". And there was good reason for his delayed response. An entry on April 5, 1944 states clearly, "I rec. this book this evening at 5 o'clock and a letter from Violet and Claudia.". (Claudia was his sister.)

    Therefore, it was through Mother's encouragement and vision that this Diary was written. And that was always true throughout their marriage. She was the one with the vision, positive outlook and plans and he was the one who got things done. Each added strength to the other and this was good for them.

Chapter Two

A Hurried "Boot Camp"

One can only begin to imagine the family events that took place between December 27, 1943 when he received the draft notice until he took the oath on January 29, 1944 to faithfully serve his country. There must have been many quiet discussions between Mother and him regarding what to do "in case of....". One of my lingering memories is how strongly Mother faced the situation. She never showed her concerns and fears to her children, although I'm sure they were there. She was firm in her faith that God was in control of her life and her husband's and she moved from day to day exhibiting that. She must have known, however, the burden that she was about to bear caring for six children between the ages of two to thirteen on the small farm with very limited income while her husband would be facing the dangers of fierce warfare in distant lands.

The time between January 29, 1944 when he was inducted and February 5 when he reported for active duty at the Navy Reserve Station at Abingdon, Virginia, must have passed all to swiftly but time passes fast when one is engaged in a great undertaking and this was one of immense proportions for them.

On February 5, 1944, he boarded a train in Abingdon to report to the Naval Training Station, Bainbridge, Maryland to undergo five weeks of "boot camp" preparation prior to being assigned his duty station.

The first entries Dad made in his diary, after receiving it in April, were backdated.

Saturday, February 5, 1944   "I left for boot camp."

<u>Sunday, February 6</u> "Arrived at Bainbridge, Md. today at 11: o'clock."

He was assigned to the 17th Battalion, Company 4052, U. S. Naval Training Station, Bainbridge Maryland, which consisted of 138 men. Anyone who has been through "boot camp" will understand why there were no entries in the Diary from February 6 until March 13 for it is a time when the company officers, platoon leaders and squad leaders control every minute of your life. In fact, this period of time becomes a blur for most who go through it except for a few highlights that remain for a lifetime. New friends, new and very different living environment and lots to learn while "surviving" a rigorous physical training schedule is the order of the day. In addition, Dad was the "old man" at 31 to the other "men" of 18, more or less.

There is, however, one small bit of information which was printed in ***The Dickensonian***, a local newspaper, dated 25 February, 1944 that gives some insight to his training camp. It reads: "And Truman Fleming, big game hunter extraordinary, writes from Bainbridge, Md. that he has taken a number of aptitude tests and that he has qualified as a marksman and will be assigned to duty on a merchant vessel as a gunman with the naval crew. Although he has been in the naval training base for something like only a couple of weeks he has been given the rank of Gunner's Mate, Third Class. The lad is going places in a hurry."

Also, assigned to the same company were three other young men whom Dad knew from Dickenson County: Gene Culbertson, Ellis Epling, Sr. and Earnest B. Colley. I was able to locate all three men's military records in the court house and discovered that all four were drafted on the same day, sworn in together, left for training together and trained in the same company. Even after basic training they shipped out together to New York and were assigned to the same Escort Division of six destroyer escorts. Their friendships grew as the Diary tells later in a series of incidents.

Company 4052 graduated on Monday, March 13, 1944 and the following entry was made in the Diary: "Left Bainbridge today on furlough from boot camp."

CO 4052 U S NAVAL TRAINING STATION
BAINBRIDGE, MARYLAND MARCH 14, 1944

Having experienced "boot camp" myself, I'm sure he left immediately for home on the very first available train because the next entry reads:

Tuesday, March 14 "Arrived in Bristol, Va. this morning at 4:15 A.M. Arrived home at 8:30 A. M."

He had traveled all night to get home to see his family. He gives no explanation why he arrived in Bristol instead of Abingdon or how he got home from Bristol. But those are minor details for a man who had been away from his wife and family for the first time in his life. In addition, because it was a time of great national crisis everyone was so willing to assist any person in uniform that it would have been easy for him to get a ride from Bristol to Abingdon or even from either to home.

It was a seven day furlough and I am sure they were happy days for Mother and him and, of course, he was a gigantic hero to his children. But, all good things must come to an end.

Truman, March, 1944

Tuesday, March 21, 1944 "Left at 11 o'clock back for O. G. U." (*O. G. U. is an abbreviation for Out Going Unit.*)

Wednesday, March 22, 1944 " Arrived in Bainbridge this morning at 10:45 A.M."

Early 1942 was a time of heavy loss of merchant ships, personnel and war materiel being shipped to Europe due to attacks by the German U-Boats (Unterseeboot) that were prowling the Atlantic coast of the United States, the Caribbean and the North Atlantic Ocean. In the brief time of April, May and June, 1942 the U-Boats sunk over 300 ships because the convoys did not have adequate destroyer escort protection.

The United States Navy therefore was placed in a position of preparing men for sea duty as rapidly as possible to meet projected needs because President Franklin D. Roosevelt had earlier approved a massive destroyer escort ship building project to be placed in the service of combating the U-Boats and escorting large convoys of ships carrying huge numbers of men and vast amounts of supplies and war materiel to Europe. The ship building project began in early 1942 and produced 563 destroyer escorts in about 1 ½ years at 6 US Navy Yards and 10 private shipyards! In fact, the projected time to place a destroyer escort into service was 32 months. But because this little fighting ship had proven to be the most effective weapon the Allies had to combat the German submarines, the actual average time to place one in service was 15 months and the record was an astounding 23 1/3 days when the USS FIEBERLING, DE 640, was commissioned by the Seth Ship Building Company, Mare Island, San Francisco, California!

In fact, the destroyer was such a new type of ship the officers and men often did not have a lot of experience operating them before being placed in command. To illustrate this point the following is taken, with permission, from a non-copy right account by William Wenzel who served as an officer aboard the USS HOPPING, DE 155/APD 51 from July 20, 1943 to October 30, 1945:

"During the next few days I became more acquainted with the officers and the ship. Tim Brin, the gunnery officer directly over me,

DESTROYER-ESCORT BUILT IN 23¹/₃ DAYS

San Francisco Yard of Bethlehem Steel Sets New All-Time Record

Building of the Destroyer-Escort Fieberling by the San Francisco Yard of Bethlehem Steel Company 231/3 days after keel-laying marks a new record for the construction of this type of combat ship.

The Fieberling, which has now taken her place as a part of the great and growing United States Navy, is a fast, powerful fighting unit. She has a main battery with guns mounted in three turrets which can revolve in a complete circle to follow a target, and can be fired with amazing speed and accuracy. She bristles with 40-MM and 20-MM guns especially for anti-aircraft work. She has numerous K-guns which can toss out the famous 300-lb. "ash cans" that crumple the sides or crack the seams of enemy submarines.

That such a ship was built and turned over to the Navy in so short a time is a tribute to the industry and enthusiasm of the employees of the San Francisco Yard, and the cooperation of employees and management, working together as an effective team. In defeating the U-Boat menace and getting the convoys through, the U.S. Navy has won a decisive victory, shaping the entire course of the war. In that accomplishment, the fleet of relentless, hard hitting destroyer-escorts has played a major role.

* * * * * * * *

Bethlehem Built 380 Ships in 1943

In 1943 Bethlehem Steel Company's Shipbuilding Division built 380 ships, including Aircraft Carriers, Cruisers, Destroyers, Destroyer-Escorts, Landing Crafts, Tankers, Liberty Ships, and other vessels.

This production is equivalent to 1000 Liberty Ships.

During the same year more than 7000 vessels were converted, repaired or serviced in Bethlehem Yards.

Submitted by Gerard Benkert

---

was a laid-back southerner who had prior duty on a merchant ship in charge of an 'armed guard' crew, (Navy gun crews aboard private merchant ships.) on the Marmansk Run, above the Arctic Circle in Russia. He had faced considerable enemy action and frigid cold and Brin had been decorated with a 'Silver Star' for his part, but had requested change of duty. Guy Wainscott, my roommate, was a graduate of UCLA. He was a handsome fellow who was easy to live with.

*Midshipman Wenzel
Columbia University
1943*

Loutrel had an engineering degree from Yale and had grown up as a yachtsman, sailing off the East Coast of Maine to Massachusetts in a variety of private sailing vessels. He was, without a doubt, the most able seaman of anyone aboard. Chief Engineering Officer, LaVerne Bordwell, who went by the name of 'Chief' (never call him "LaVerne"!) was a 'mustang'. That is, he had been an enlisted man (He told me it was a choice between joining the circus or the Navy and he chose the Navy.) who earned his way up to Chief Petty Officer and when the war started he was appointed an Ensign. The Captain and Chief Bordwell were the only regular Navy (USN) officers aboard. The rest of us were Navy Reserve (USNR) who had gone through midshipmen school for ninety days to earn our commissions. In addition to the captain who was a lieutenant commander, there were three full lieutenants, three lieutenant jgs., and four ensigns; a total of eleven officers at the time. There were one hundred eighty-eight men on the 'muster' list, among whom were seven Chief Petty Officers and seventeen first class petty officers, the next rating below 'chief'. These, the chiefs and the first class petty officers, were the backbone of the ship. They had experience and expertise in their specialties. The officers really had to rely on these top rated men. Obviously, they knew more in their specific fields than we did. For most of us, it was on-the-job training. Probably eighty percent of the crew, officers and men, had never been to sea before. Many of the unrated seamen aboard were from sixteen to eighteen years in age, eager, inexperienced, young men. The ensigns were just out of college and in their twenties, the jgs. a year or so older; add a year or two for each higher rank. We were all young!!"

Since the destroyer escorts were being commissioned at a rapid pace by mid 1943 the need for about 112,600 men to put these ships into action was urgent. Therefore, basic training was sped up but it must have been more than adequate because it has been said by military historians that the destroyer escorts played a major roll in turning the tide of the war in favor of the Allied Forces because of their effectiveness against the German submarines which allowed the convoys to arrive safely in Europe to support the massive build up of troops and supplies for the invasion that occurred on D-Day, June 6, 1944. And there is more than adequate evidence from captured German submariners and German ships' records to substantiate the fear and destructive toll the "trim but deadly" destroyer escorts inflicted on the German navy from 1943 until the war ended in Europe. It is reported that in the final two years of the war in Europe the Germans lost over 27,000 U-Boat officers and men and it was the highest loss rate of any unit of their armed forces.

Such were the time and need for men and ships to perform in combat situations and the crews and ships certainly did!

Chapter Three

Delayed Assignment

Saturday, March 25 "Left this morning at 2 o'clock A. M. for New York. Arrived here at 12:30 P. M. on a troop train. Had a G. I. hair cut this morning.".

No explanation is offered in the Diary as to why it took 10 ½ hours to travel from Baltimore, Maryland to New York City. However, in an interview Robert O. Davidson from Rogersville, TN, said that there was so much train traffic going into and out of New York City at this time that a troop train spent a lot of time on the side tracks waiting for other trains to pass. At least that is what he experienced going from Bainbridge, Maryland to New York City at approximately the same time that Dad made the trip.

Sunday, March 26 "We were issued our Billit & assigned our ship. And it was the U. S. S. HOPPING, D. E. 155."

The following excerpt is taken from the "Dictionary of American Naval Fighting Ships," (1969) Vol. 4, p. 363 regarding the HOPPING:

"The U. S. S. HOPPING, (DE-155; Displacement: 1,400 tons; Length: 306'; Beam: 36' 10"; Draft: 9'5"; Speed: 24 knots; Complement: 186; Armament: 3, 3"; 4, 1.1"; 8, 20mm.; 2 depth charge tracks; 8 depth charge projectors; 1 hedge hog; Class - Buckley).

HOPPING (DE-155) was launched by Norfolk Navy Yard, Portsmouth, Virginia, 9 March 1943; sponsored by Mrs. H. L. Hopping, widow of Lieutenant Commander Hopping; and commissioned 21 May 1943, Lt. Commander F. D. Giambatista in command.

Lt. Cmdr. Hallstead L. Hopping

The new destroyer escort conducted shakedown training out of Bermuda and after escorting an LST convoy to Norfolk made a voyage to Casablanca, where she arrived 2 September 1943. There HOPPING formed a new convoy and returned to New York 25 September.

In the year that followed, HOPPING made nine convoy crossings from New York to United Kingdom ports, bringing vital supplies for the war in Europe."

Commissioning Officer

Rear Admiral Felix Gygax, U. S. N.
Commandant, Norfolk Navy Yard

Sponsor

Mrs. Hallsted L. Hopping

ROSTER OF OFFICERS, U. S. S. HOPPING (DE-155)

1. Commanding Officer   Lt. Comdr. F. D. Giambattista, USN.
2. Executive Officer   Lt. L. F. Loutrel, USNR.
3. Gunnery Officer   Lt. R. T. Brinn, USNR.
4. First Lieutenant   Lt. D. A. Benson, USNR.
5. Communication Officer   Lt. (jg) G. Wainscott, Jr., USNR.
6. Electrical Officer   Lt. (jg) E. T. Hargrave, Jr., USNR.
7. Asst. First Lieutenant   Lt. (jg) J. D. Evans, USNR.
8. Engineering Officer   Ens. L. A. Bordwell, USN.
9. Asst. Gunnery Officer   Ens. A. R. Brown, USNR.
10. A. S. W. Officer   Ens. R. E. Wood, USNR.

Order of Events

PRELIMINARY MUSIC BY BAND

1. The Commanding Officer meets the Commandant at the side.
2. The Commanding Officer reports to the Commandant that all is in readiness for commissioning ceremony.
3. The Commandant and party proceed to Quarterdeck and the Commandant orders Bugler to sound ATTENTION.
4. The Commandant refers to the directive from the Navy Department for commissioning the ship.
5. The Commandant directs the Commanding Officer to issue necessary orders for all hands to face FORWARD.
6. The Commandant orders "SOUND COLORS".
   National Anthem played by band, National Ensign, Jack hoisted and commission pennant broken. Admiral's flag replaces commission pennant immediately, if desired.
7. The Commanding Officer faces crew to front.
8. The Commandant asks Chaplain to offer invocation.
9. The Commandant makes brief address and turns ship over to the Commanding Officer.
10. The Commanding Officer (facing crew), reads his orders to command and assumes command.
11. The Commanding Officer directs "SET THE WATCH".
12. Presentation of Yard representatives with Co-op Gift.
13. Congratulations — The Commandant may inspect ship — The Commandant leaves ship — Honors may be rendered.

U. S. S. Hopping

The U. S. S. HOPPING is named in honor of Lieutenant Commander HALLSTED L. HOPPING, U. S. N., and is the first destroyer to be so named.

Lieutenant Commander HOPPING was born in New York City, September 2, 1902. He was appointed to the Naval Academy from the Nineteenth District of New York in 1920 and was graduated and commissioned Ensign in 1924. He was advanced to Lieutenant (jg) in 1927, Lieutenant in 1932 and Lieutenant Commander in 1938.

After graduation he served on the U. S. S. RICHMOND for two years and, in August, 1926, reported to the Naval Air Station, Pensacola, Florida, for flight training, upon completion of that course in November, 1927, he served in the Aircraft Squadrons, Scouting Fleet, until May, 1930, when he reported to the Naval Air Station, Coco Solo, Canal Zone, in August 1932, he was transferred to the Fleet Air Base, Coco Solo. He was under postgraduate instruction in general line duties at the Naval Academy from May, 1933, to May, 1934, when he joined the U. S. S. LANGLEY. In May 1936, he was transferred to the U. S. S. RANGER and, later, to the U. S. S. NEW ORLEANS. In June, 1937, he reported as Officer in Command of the Naval Reserve Aviation Base, Minneapolis, Minnesota. He was detached from that duty in November, 1938, and served at the Naval Air Station, San Diego, California, until June 1939, when he assumed command of a Scouting Squadron attached to a Carrier.

Lieutenant Commander HOPPING was killed in enemy action of February 1, 1942. The following letter of commendation was awarded him posthumously:

> "For distinguished service in line of his profession as Commanding Officer of a Scouting Squadron during the operations of United States Forces against enemy land bases. Lieutenant Commander HOPPING led his squadron from an Aircraft Carrier in an air attack on Enemy land bases. Despite poor visibility due to semi-darkness, as well as fighter opposition and heavy anti-aircraft fire, the attack was made in a most effective manner which resulted in considerable loss to the enemy, although it also resulted in the loss of Lieutenant Commander HOPPING'S life when his plane was shot down. For your praiseworthy conduct on this occasion, you are hereby commended."

Mrs. Hallsted L. Hopping, the sponsor of the U. S. S. HOPPING is the widow of Lieutenant Commander HALLSTED L. HOPPING.

War Widow Is Head Of Navy Housing Plan

Helps Men's Families To Get Settled Here
—Lists Many Vacancies

The listing for apartments available for navy men are not coming in fast enough for Mrs. Halisted Hopping, in charge of the housing program at the Brooklyn Navy Yard. Navy men pour in daily to her office and the conversation runs something like this:

"My wife and little boy are arriving on the train tonight to spend a few weeks with me. Will you find a place where we can stay?"

Mrs. Hopping, who followed the fleet for 16 years herself, knows exactly what navy men are up against in a strange town. Her husband, Lt. Comdr. Halisted Hopping, was killed in the first raider attack on Marshall Island last February. She tried to be with her husband every time he was on shore—even if it meant pawning some jewelry to get the fare.

Mrs. Hopping goes through some routine questions when interviewing the seaman who wants living quarters. She wants to know how many rooms and beds are needed. She wants to know how much the applicant can afford to pay and how long his family plans to be in Brooklyn.

Has Card File

Then she thumbs through the cards she has on file. If the card is for a new landlady, she or one of her assistants go out and inspect the apartment or rooms to see if they fit the requirements. Frequently she has an applicant for an apartment before another navy tenant moves out.

This navy wife has been head of the housing bureau at the navy yard since Dec. 8 last when it was formed. Although she was born in Brooklyn, her 16 years of migratory life made her feel like Rip Van Winkle when she returned here two months after her husband's death. She compiled her first list of rooms by actually hunting down apartments. She walked streets and knocked at the doors of likely houses. She was amazed at the co-operation she received from home owners.

Mrs. Halisted Hopping

Finding apartments is only one of the problems to be solved by Mrs. Hopping. She gets requests every day for baby carriages, diaper services, linen rentals, ration books and ticket information.

"If a man comes in some day and asks where he can get a boa constrictor I won't be the least bit surprised. I know I can call the zoo. I expect them to ask for anything," she says, cheerfully.

Relied on Phone

"When the unusual requests first started to come in I was constantly consulting the phone book. I now have a pretty complete list of telephone numbers but I never seem to be one jump ahead of the navy."

Mrs. Hopping wants to get into the Waves if she can. She feels that with her navy background she has something real to offer. Her main problem is her five-year-old daughter, Carol, who now lives with Mrs. Hopping and her mother at 161 Henry St.

USS HOPPING, DE 155

Dad's diary continues in New York City:

Monday, March 27 "My first liberty was granted this evening at 7 P. M. I went out to explore the wonder city, New York, a bit. Found it to be a new experience."

Tuesday, March 28 "I had a trip to Bayonne, N. J. today. Saw the Statue of Liberty for my first time. Also, saw some large ships."

Wednesday, March 29 "On liberty again tonite, walked downtown all alone to explore as usual. Sent Mama a nice pillow top. Also a Easter greeting. Also found one that I sent my wife. I sure think they are nice. W.T.F."

Thursday, March 30 "On a working party down at Pier 45 until 3:30 P. M."

Friday, March 31 "Back at pier 45 today."

Saturday, April 1 "Liberty again. Earnest B. Colley and me had our pictures snapped at the Hurricane."

Sunday, April 2 "Mailed our photos home this morning."

Monday, April 3 "This morning we fell out on the drill field and marched as the band played & the colors marched by."

Truman Fleming and Earnest Colley,

Tuesday, April 4 "I was on the U. S. S. Camden. I rec. this book this evening at 5 o'clock & a letter from Violet and Claudia."

Wednesday, April 5 "We mustered inside on top deck but did not have any detail until this afternoon. And 30 of us were sent to the spud room to cut potatoes & clean celery for next day. Earnest B. Colley, Stanley J. Figiel and me were working at the same tub, did we have us some fun. Also had a nice mess of horse stew for supper chow. Ho, Ho!"

Thursday, April 6 "I had exercise until 11 o'clock. Took a shower, then ate chow. Was due liberty, instead I wrote letters, one to Claudia, one to Thurston Meade, one to Evering Countiss. I also had a nice rest on my bunk. The boys that were in boots with me at Bainbridge left today at noon on the U. S. S. Brown (DE-258), a Destroyer E. (Raymond Bartley, Louis Albright, Alfred Black & others.) I am expecting my ship in any time. Also a telegram!"

The subject of this telegram will be discussed later in the diary.

Friday, April 7 "Today I was on the U.S.S. Camden until 10:30 a. m.

Then I had chow. All evening I walked around hoping to get a letter from someone.

This evening I rec. a letter from Violet wrote Mon. Nite, April 3, 44. Also, one from Claudia. Violet rec. her second check that day, Mon., Apr. 3, 1944.

I am lying on my bunk now just wandering what you are doing & all and how long it will be until I will be back home.

Wrote three letters. Violet, Claudia, Charlie Sowards."

It is easy to tell from this last entry that boredom was becoming a factor while waiting around for his ship to arrive and the feeling of loneliness for wife and family was beginning to affect him. Any person who has ever served in the military will vouch for the fact that the lack of letters from home is the thing they miss the most. Especially, as in Dad's situation, when the knowledge of such uncertain and impending dangers lurked ahead. Also, the Diary reveals that, in addition to receiving regular letters from Mother, he received many letters from his sister, Claudia, some other family members and from a few close friends. Dad was always a friendly, gregarious person. Therefore, the many letters to and from his family and friends must have been a comfort to him and a source of sharing his inner feelings with trusted ones. To my knowledge there are none of the letters remaining today.

While Dad was awaiting arrival of his ship in New York, the Hopping was returning from its fifth convoy escort duty to Europe.

According to the ship's WAR DIARY FOR APRIL 1944: *"Entered New York on 6 April, 1944 at 1108 hours, swept channel, steering various courses and patrolling port side of convoy now formed in column, open order. At 1421, passed net and anchored in Gravesend Bay at 1427 to unload ammunition. Underway for Navy Yard at 1540 and at 1702, moored, berth 17, Navy Yard, New York for 10 days post voyage availability."*

The Hopping had been at sea for over a year now with five escort crossings and had faced many dangerous situations during that time. One such crossing, the fourth, is certainly worthy of note. During this trip, six days out of Londonderry on her way to New York, she encountered what became known in the annals of Navy records as the "Christmas Hurricane of 1943".

On Christmas Day the convoy hit a hurricane with sustained winds reaching 70 to 80 miles per hour and lasting two days. It must have been a very difficult task keeping the slow moving convoy together while screening for German U-Boats and ushering stragglers who were experiencing engine or other troubles back to the convoy when waves were so large the ship would often disappear in the trough between the crest of the waves.. This trip, which normally would take ten days, took nineteen days from Londonderry to New York. A first hand account of this terrific storm can be found in TEMPEST, FIRE & FOE, by Lewis M. Andrews, Jr., 1999, pages 23 and 24. Andrews was the Executive Officer aboard the USS SIMS, DE-154, which was part of the six ship escort division along with the Hopping.

USS HOPPING DE 155, Sept. 1943, Brooklyn Navy Yard

The next fifteen months that lay ahead for Dad, the crew of the Hopping and the crews of the five other destroyer escorts of Escort Division Six is a story of bravery and sacrifice that needs to be told and preserved for the sake and memory of those who endured and suffered the horrors of World War II aboard these fighting ships in both the Atlantic and Pacific theaters.

Dad's wait to board the USS HOPPING, DE 155 was about to end and more new experiences lay ahead.

Chapter Four

On Board and Training Exercises

Saturday, April 8 "Assigned to the U. S. Hopping, D. E. 155. Went aboard her at 5:30 P. M. Had chow then went to the movies. I had a surprise when I came aboard. I sat down to chow and a young man came in and was talking to us. I asked him if he was Wallenfelts. He replied, 'Yes. Are you Fleming?' 'Sure.' My cousin! Great to meet a cousin at sea, such as this. He is Fred Wallenfelts from Roanoke, Va." (Correct spelling is *Wallenfelsz.)*

"Bought my watch today, $25.75. T.F."

Sunday, April 9 "Easter Sunday. Taps 0700.

For breakfast, two fried, coffee, cereal, sausage, apples & fruit. Went to Catholic Church. Had chow at 1200, chicken, mashed potatoes, gravy, can beans, ice cream, coffee.

This is a nice home, I think. W. T. F."

Monday, April 10 "We moved out to dry dock today. Stood guard on fantail."

Tuesday, April 11 "Chipped paint until 2:45 then took a shower & dressed to leave for Long Island for gunnery school. Mr. Lee Emgee brought us four pies & one box of donuts."

Wednesday, April 12 "Left 5:30 for practice. Practiced until 10:30 & out for chow. Chicken for chow. Back for drill to 3:30, then back to hotel to write. Here sure is a beautiful place.

This is the beautifulest hotel I've ever seen. Hotel Nassau on the boardwalk, Long Beach, Long Island, N.Y.

This was written at 3:45 P. M. on 5th floor, Room #12. Epling, Dowless Warren, Dooley, Evans, Fielder, Figiel, Eidson - room mates here."

Thursday, April 13 "I was on gun practice today shooting 20 M.M. Went on liberty & wrote Mom & Violet. Went to U. S. O. & St. James service men's club. I like the 20 M. M. practice. Fired 80 shots & made 240. My instructor said 'Dam good!' so I am well pleased with that. I am sitting here on my bunk looking out over the Atlantic Ocean. It sure is pretty. I can see for miles. It looks like it turns over the hill just as a ball looks. We will leave tomorrow evening at four o'clock for Brooklyn, N. Y. to our ship. I would like to be at home now but let's win this Victory & Stand by "Old Glory" - the one and only. W.T.F."

The preceding statement accurately depicts the willingness and attitude of nearly every person in the United States during this most difficult period. It was this attitude that the enemy soon learned to fear because they were fighting for a cause greater than themselves and one they willingly gave their complete and undivided effort to attain victory. Probably never before in the history of mankind has a nation and its people come together as quickly with as much commitment to defend its belief and achieved so much in less time. Those in uniform did not and still do not see themselves as heroes; instead they simply understood their job, set themselves to the task and did what they had to do without expectation of recognition. President George W. Bush said it best in his dedication speech of the D-Day Memorial, Bedford, VA on June 6, 2001, "They did not yearn to be heroes - they yearned for summer nights and harvest time." It is clear this is what my father yearned for but was willing to give it his best as he contributed to the effort of " let's win this Victory & Stand by 'Old Glory' - the one and only."

Many, even most, would not discuss their wartime experiences upon returning because they were so unpleasant and horrible it was too painful and as one veteran said to me in 2003, "I didn't discuss it with my folks because they could not understand what it was like because they had not experienced it". My father was no exception; yet he was very proud to have served his country and to have given his small part to the victory. He remained very patriotic until his death in 1958 and instilled in his family a strong sense of duty, loyalty and service to the United States.

Friday, April 14 "7:20 in the morning. We will leave this afternoon for our ship. 7:25 p.m. I have just read my mail and had chow. We got back to our ship at 6 o'clock. I shot 4 rounds today and scored the highest, so they all said. We are ready to have a show now, so I'll finish. I rated liberty tonite but will not go out. Our ship is out of dry dock. Came out this afternoon sometime."

Saturday, April 15 "Today we loaded supplies, two big truck loads. Getting ready to shove off. Went to the movies. It was about boxing altogether - from the first of boxing to the present time. Went to bed at 9:30 and slept until 7 o'clock Sun. Morning. Sure slept good, too."

Sunday, April 16 "This morning I was eating chow and was called to the Exect's Office. I rec. a telegram, but too late. We are shoving off tomorrow morning sometime, to sea! I rec. a letter from Violet telling me she got the pillow top & when she read the verse on it she cried. Well, I think it was the sweetest verse & top I ever saw. Sure hope I can see you all soon but have a long journey in front of me. I got letters from Donald (*Dotson, brother-in-law*), Lucille (*Mullins, sister-in-law*). Virgil (*Fleming, cousin*), Violet and Charlie Sowards (*close friend and WW I combat veteran*). I also drew pay today - $32.00. I sure need it. I only have .36 cents. Ho, Ho. Almost broke. It is raining today."

Monday, April 17 "At 8:30 off for maneuvers, at 9:30 took on ammunition. Off again at 11. Anchored at 12 for chow, then off again at 4:30. Hit out to sea at 5:30, the water looks pretty & green. D. E. 54 (D. T. Griffin) fell in ahead of us at 6:15. We sailed all nite. Had chow at 7:30, and on again. I was on watch from 8 to 12 on gun #4, 1 point 1, 75 M.M. Me & Maimone & two more boys slept in hammock tonite. It slept pretty good."

Tuesday, April 18 "We were off at 8 o'clock and were getting ready for Capt.'s inspection all day until 11:30 P. M. We anchored tonite in the sea near Long Island or Mantok, Conn. one. We just cruised around today all day again. Store opened at 6:30 & I bought a carton of Luckies for

.50 cents and a box of double mint gum for .70 cents - 10 pkgs."

The ship's WAR DIARY FOR APRIL 1944 gave the following account for April 18:

"0505   Entered area Nan south of Montauk point. All ships exercising independently calibrating compasses and MF/DF equipment.

1550   Forming columns open order and proceeding on various courses to anchorage at Fort Pond Bay, Montauk, New York.

1856 Anchored in Fort Pond Bay."

Wednesday, April, 19   "We were off at 8 A. M. and on maneuvers all day. It is 6:15 and we are still going. I ate supper at 5:30. We chased a sub. all day. It was a large one. It did 20 knots a while this morning. We maneuvered all nite. Chased P. T.'s until 11:30 tonite then secured and went to bed. It sure was cold above deck. Another new experience for me."

The ship's WAR DIARY FOR APRIL 1944 gave this account of April, 19:

"0643   Underway for training exercises.

0812   Commenced exercises with USS BARRACUDA in company with USS CHARLES LAWRENCE (DE-53) and USS DONNELL (DE-56).

1530   Completed submarine runs.

1700   Formed scouting line with all ships of CortDiv 6. Steaming on various courses enroute to PT exercise area.

2030   Commenced exercise with PT boats continuing until 2315.

2330   Standing out Narragansett swept channel with ships of Cort Div 6."

Thursday, April 20   "Revilee at 6:30. Chow at 7:00 and off at sea for firing drill. We began firing at 2:30. Ceased at 3:45 then off for anchor. Anchored at 5:30 at Point Monticello, Long Island. I ate chow at 5:45. I was second loader on the 1 point 1, 75 MM. Hudson was my 1st loader.

We put out the most rounds, 6-7-8-9 rounds shooting at sleeves pulled by a plane. I also had a good hot shower this evening. Boy, a 3 inch 50 caliber sure does crack. It rings in my ears all the time. Big Chief Logan was on it, a Indian. This sure has been a thrill to me. We will head for New York tomorrow morning, 21st. A new experience on the 1 point 1 75 M.M. Myself, Rebel, Maimone, Hudson and about 8 more boys standing by. Around 16 men for a crew."

The WAR DIARY FOR APRIL 20 reads:

"0700 *Detached with USS Reeves (DE-156) for exercises with French submarine Argo.*

0830 *Commenced exercises conducting two ship creeping attacks.*

1200 *Turned over services of submarine to USS CHARLES LAWRENCE and departed for AA firing area.*

1350 *to 1430 Conducting AA firing with USS REEVES.*

1545 *Departed from area for Fort Pond Bay.*

1730 *Anchored in Fort Pond Bay.*

Friday, April 21 "We were off this morning at 7 for more firing. We fired from 1:30 until 4 this afternoon, then off for Staten Island. We arrived in Staten Island about 8. I was on watch from 8 - 12. I slept good when I got in sack.

Maggie's (*Roberts, half-sister*), Grandpa's (*George Fleming, paternal grandfather*), & Tandy's (*Fleming, great uncle*) birthday."

The ship's WAR DIARY FOR APRIL 21:

"0648 *Underway for training exercises.*

0850 *Commenced A/S exercises with French submarine Argo. USS DONNELL and USS REEVES.*

1230 *Turned over submarine Argo to USS CHARLES LAWRENCE, departed in company with USS DONNELL and USS REEVES for firing area.*

1400 Commenced surface firing practice exercising all 3" 50 guns at local control practice.

1615 Completed firing.

1800 Rendezvous with all ship of CortDiv 6. Formed scouting line on course 237 degree T. Proceeding to point Zebra."

The aforementioned quotes from the WAR DIARY FOR APRIL 1944 are presented to show the accuracy of Dad's observations from the viewpoint of a seaman. The diary continues to demonstrate this accuracy throughout as from time-to-time will be pointed out for verification, authenticity and information.

Saturday, April 22 "Billy's birthday, 12 years. (*Second son*) We pulled in dock at 8 o'clock this morning. Our convoy is here with us. I awoke this morning going into dock with our convoy at Staten Island. We have a large convoy. I am looking to leave out about Monday. I got a letter from Dan (*Crabtree, father-in-law*) and two from Claudia & two from Violet and one from Cat (*Catherine Branham, niece*). Claudia sure wrote me a sad letter. Tears came in my eyes. I am well & fat, doing fine. T.F."

I am sure the "sad" letter Aunt Claudia wrote was about her separation and eventual divorce from her first husband, Orville Branham. Cat was their daughter, so her letter was probably about the same subject. She was about 13 years old at this time and went to live with our grandmother, Minerva Fleming, until she graduated from high school and went to Emory & Henry College where she graduated with honors.

Sunday, April 23 "I wrote Violet, Mom, D.R. (*Daniel Robert Crabtree, father-in-law*) today as I was sitting in the movie locker room. We had turkey for dinner. I ate a whole leg. Epling took sick at noon and I packed his gear & took him to the ambulance, sent him to U. S. N. Hospital at Brooklyn, N. Y. Then I got liberty & went over in Manhatten, got back at 2400 midnite. I hated to see Epling leave for we had been together all through boots & O. G. U & Pier 92 & separated today but Doc told us not worry we would be together next trip. That helped us up a lot. Claudia's birthday, 29 years."

I was able to locate Ellis Epling, Jr. in The Breaks, Virginia to confirm his father's illness. He said his father had mentioned many times before he died in 1962 that he had appendicitis and had to go to the hospital in New York to have his appendix removed, therefore, the reason for leaving the ship at this time. (The ship's personnel log confirms this 'transfer for treatment' on April 23.)

Just as Dad had stated on April 22, Monday would be the day they embarked. The training was over for the Hopping and five other destroyer escorts, CHARLES LAWRENCE, DE 53; SIMS, DE 154; REEVES, DE 156; DONNELL, DE 56; and D. T. GRIFFIN, DE 54. They were now prepared to take on the task of escorting a large convoy of ships to Europe. They formed what was called a convoy escort division, CortDiv 6. Their responsibility was to deliver their charges safely to port in Londonderry, Northern Ireland.

Individual German submarines as well as "Wolf Packs" were very much on the prowl in the Atlantic Ocean searching for convoys to attack to reduce the number of men and materiel being sent to the Allied Forces in Europe. So one can only begin to imagine what was on Dad's mind as well as all men who were about to face the daunting task of getting another convoy safely through the treacherous waters of the North Atlantic.

Chapter Five

Forming A Convoy And Escort Duty

Sunday, April 24 "This morning at 8 o'clock we left Staten Island for Ireland & elsewhere. We got our convoy together around three this afternoon. It has rained all day on us. It is 4:10 now. I hated to start before I got to see my folks. Hope I get to spend my 14th anniversary at home. June 23, 1930, I was married and I'm sure proud of my gal "Violet". Ho Ho!

Sure hope I return to her. I sure could be happy with you and kids & Mother. Could I enjoy myself!"

The WAR DIARY OF APRIL 1944 recorded on April 24 at 0926:

"Underway from berth at Pier 10 together with other ships of TG 21.6 as escorts for convoy CU-22 in accordance, CinClants 171423 of April. Routing as per Port Director, N. Y., N. Y.'s Serial USN #98 of April 1944. At 1515 Took departure from Bouy "A" at point Zebra. Convoy forming up on base course 121 degree T., 8 knots in heavy fog. Identifying ships of convoy and furnishing the information to assist in forming cruising order. 2000 hours, 32 ships in convoy partially formed in 7 columns, speed 8 knots. Took screening station #2 ahead of convoy."

Some entries from the WAR DIARY for April 25 thru 28 offer insight into the challenges of forming a convoy just out of port and getting it prepared for the long crossing ahead. The Hopping must have been the lead destroyer for the escorts because on April 25 an entry reads:

"'0300 Directed ship believed to be #11 to decrease speed as he was 8

miles ahead.' and '0530 Lost radar contact with ship ahead of convoy.' 'The HOPPING left convoy to search for the ship in heavy fog and the convoy was widely scattered. Three hours later it rejoined the convoy and the results of the search for the "lost" ship was negative. At 1100 hours 24 ships now formed the convoy with other groups nearby. At 1515, a British ship, HMS RULER joined the main body of the convoy and at 1630 the convoy increased speed to 14 knots. At 1745 the SIMS and REEVES joined with group.'

'On April 26 at 0520 the GRIFFIN and LAWRENCE left screening stations to count convoy. One ship, SS ROBIN LOCKSLEY, not accounted for and two others having returned to New York because of engine trouble.' ' At 1501 radar contact was made with a ship at 23 miles. The HOPPING was ordered by CTG 21.6, the convoy command ship, to investigate. It was the SS ROBIN LOCKSLEY. It was escorted to station #65 in the convoy.'

'On April 27 at 0001 clocks were set ahead one hour to zone plus three time. 0100 made radar contact at 13 ½ miles. REEVES ordered to investigate. The convoy executed 45 degree turn to left to avoid radar contact and then 45 degree right. The REEVES identified the ship as a U. S. Coast Guard vessel. The convoy consisted of 32 ships in seven columns.'

'April 28 was refueling day for the escorts and the convoy changed speed to 12 knots to accomplish this. The Hopping completed fueling at 0934 with 18,774 gallons.' "

Until May 3 the Hopping's WAR DIARY OF APRIL 1944 shows rather routine convoy escort duty.

In a separate Confidential, Report of Operations, the Commander of Task Group 21.6 presented the following to The Commander in Chief, United States Fleet regarding the formation of Convoy CU-22: "Convoy CU-22 escorted by Task Group TWENTY-ONE POINT SIX (Destroyer, Escort Division SIX) with addition of U. S. S. Chemung sailing in the convoy, departed seaward end of swept channel beginning 1500/24 April, 1944. An attempt was made to form up on course 121 degree T, speed 8 knots but due to heavy fog, rain, and poor communication, convoy became scattered in groups. At 1500/25 April, 1944 was able to form convoy generally and increase speed. STE CHURUBUSCO did not sail, SS's BLUE JACKET and CANYON CREEK returned to New York due to machinery casualties and ROBIN LOCKSLEY did not locate and join until 1600/26 April, 1944. All ships of convoy (as modified above) arrived at Latitude 55 degrees - 30'00"N, Longitude 07 degrees - 50'-00"W at 1416/5 May, 1944, at which point they were turned over to HMS TAVY for escort to destinations. Convoy originally consisted of thirty-five (35) ships, but with three (3) dropping out as noted above, thirty-two (32) ships arrived at local escort rendezvous point. Convoy was disposed in seven (7) columns, 4, 4, 5, 5, 5, 5, 4, distance between columns 1,000 yards and distance between ships in column 600 yards. Formation speed 14 knots. Escorts were disposed in accordance with table 13 FTP 215 until torpedoing of U. S. S. DONNELL (DE-56)."

Dad gives his account of the convoy forming and what it was like for him during his first experience at sea on the USS HOPPING as his Diary continues.

Tuesday, April 25 "Today sure is a bad day, foggy and stormy, some awful bad rolls. We must be something like 300 miles out or more."

Wednesday, April 26 "I was on watch from 4 - 8 this morning. It came day about 5:30. At 6 the sun came up. It sure looked good. And was the first sun I ever saw come up on water, some 500 miles out, I suppose. We are doing around 18 knots. Its pretty blue out here. Ho Ho!"

Thursday, April 27 "We had radar contact with a lima ship last nite. Ships changed their course at 12 o'clock. This is 4 days & nites in route to Ireland. Approximately 1/3 the way, about 1200 miles from N. Y. We had gun fire today. About 18 knots now. It is 6:10 P. M. I've just ate chow. It is still good chow. On watch from 8 - 12 tonite. The clock went around one hour last nite at 11 o'clock. Jumped from 11 to 12. Sounds funny. Ho!"

Friday, April 28 "On watch from 8 - 12 today. We fired six rounds this morning and refueled from a Navy tanker at 10 knots. Fish for dinner today. This is our fifth day with five more to go to Ireland. The sea is calm today and a little cloudy. No sun much at all. It is warming up a lot. Hope it is pretty back home! For farmers. I hope I am not midway the ocean this time next year. I hope it's home. T. F."

Saturday, April 29 "Today has been cloudy, but very little sun. I am wandering what you all are doing as I sail the briney deep. We had G. Q. (General Quarters/Battle Stations) but did not fire. Also got contact with a sub but lost it. Is everyone well? I'm just wondering. The sea is calm and pretty."

Sunday, April 30 "I was on watch from 12 - 4 last nite. We were looking for trouble all nite. Now it is 1 o'clock and has been a beautiful day, sunshine & clear, but all you can see is water & the sky. I saw some several fish this morning (Porpus). This evening I saw two small whales & several flying fish. My first. I am just off watch. I have been wondering all day what "you" are doing and if you would enjoy my company. Oh! How happy I'd be if I were home now to help feed and get wood for you. The water is green as grass out here. We will get to Ireland Thursday. We are on a sharp look out by some means today. I sure wondered today (WHY?). Chicken for dinner & good, too."

I'll never forget today, how lonesome I was and what a beautiful day it is this far out in the Atlantic Ocean. The clock is three hrs. ahead now. It is 4 o'clock and is one back home. Tonite would be mine if I were at home. Ho! Ho! But I am ok! sweetheart, just as you last seen me! (Love)."

Monday, May 1 "Today has been calm out here and plenty turtles & fish. We had two or three contacts today but didn't amount to anything. Just expecting any minute. We will arrive about Thurs. Nite if no bad luck. It is 7:50 now our time. The clock went up another hour last nite at midnite. We are 3 hrs. faster than New York & 4 hrs. faster than at home now. I was changed to gun 12, 20 M.M. today at 4 P. M. for my battle station. I will hit the sack now.".

Tuesday, May 2 "Today has been cloudy. This morn. was the first time I have seen anything but ships in 9 days. Planes came out controlling about 6 o'clock this morning. Made me feel pretty good. We will port Friday morning if no bad luck. I just heard at chow that 14 German subs were out. The report came from Ireland. Makes us feel kindly shaky. I was on watch from 4 - 8 this morning & 4 - 6 this evening. I've just ate chow. Had liver & gravy. It was good, too. I'll go on watch at 12 tonite and watch for subs. Saw a big shark this morning & a Portuguese Man O War. It is 6:50 P.M. Guess you all are planting corn now. Love."

The relative calm that has been described in the Diary, the ship's WAR DIARY and the Commander's Report of T. G. 21.6 and the peace that had been experienced thus far on the journey was about to come to a startling end with the first encounter of the dreaded German submarine that, except for radar, was hidden from sight. And once again the effectiveness, efficiency and fire power of the fighting destroyer escorts, as well as the skilled seamanship of the entire crew, would be put to the ultimate test and would, once again, prove their worthiness.

Chapter Six

Imagine Seeing You Here!

Wednesday, May 3 "The Donnell was hit this morning at 10 o'clock! I saw it go up! We were fired at twice but dodged them. We turned and went after them, dropped six patterns & damaged them someway. They never did come to surface. We hunted until 8 o'clock & went screening for the Reeves as she towed the Donnell. Five or six days to go. Sure is a day to be remembered by me - fighting a German sub 250 ft. long but we got it and are we proud."

Another eyewitness account of the events of this day was captured by, Willis "Bill" C. Dailey, S 2/C, aboard the USS HOPPING in a letter he addressed to his parents in Oneonta, NY and is used with his permission. It reads:

"May 3, 1944

Well, I must say – Hello! And might I add that I hope you had a nice day today. I know of some that had a horrible experience today so I'll try to give you a candid account of it. Our plan of the day had Field Day and Captain's Inspection listed and we were well underway preparing our cleaning stations for this inspection when the word came over the TBS – "We have a very good contact bearing 058, 2300 yards." from the USS DONNELL. I was in the chart house at the time scrubbing down bulk heads. About the same time our general alarm was sounded so I was right at my battle station. Soon after that first word from the Donnell, she reported periscope off port bow and then came the explosion. When the smoke had cleared & we could see her again - the whole fantail (stern of ship) was blown right out of the water. Of course, I didn't see this until later because I'm on the inside during general quarters. However, we got the straight dope over the TBS.

The Donnell was crippled - hit in the screws by one of the acoustic torpedoes. Naturally, as we were the DE closest to our mates (the Donnell is a DE - one of our Division), we immediately came to port at full speed to see if we could help.

Our sound men were really on the ball for they made contact & we made five depth charge and hedgehog runs on those heinies. They were beautiful runs but we failed to bring her up. We did get a couple oil slicks, but that's all.

In the meantime the convoy had moved on unharmed leaving us and the USS REEVES to standby to help the Donnell. It was almost dusk when we made the last run on the sub.

The Donnell remained afloat due to watertight compartmentation but her captain had to report the sad news that 27 men were dead or missing and 20 injured. I could hardly believe it. To think we had been so close to it all, about 2 miles.

All we could do now is just circle the Donnell keeping a careful search so that no more trouble could come to her. The Reeves & da Mighty Hopping kept vigilant guard that night.

P. S. During our first runs on the sub, we escaped the fate of the Donnell by narrowly missing two torpedoes. By putting on hard right rudder and coming to flank speed one torpedo passed along our port side and the FXR gear did its intended job."

Dad's Diary continues.

Thursday, May 4 "We had a 5 o'clock Reveille this morning. Boy it sure is tough going out here. Just one ship and 14 subs shooting at you, (OH BOY). We are 600 miles from land. It is 10 o'clock now so I'll tell the story some day. 27 were killed & 24 seriously ill. Boy, is it tough going."

Friday, May 5 "I was on watch from 4 - 8 this morning. It is still rough. We are towing the Donnell at 1 knot. Two lima ships joined us last nite. It is 8:45 now and tugs are coming to get the Donnell and does that make us feel good. We got the sub, at least. We had another contact about 2 o'clock today. It sure is plenty tough but I feel better now."

Saturday, May 6 "This morning finds us still towing the Donnell. About 500 miles from Londonderry, Ireland but tugs have come to get it and we are taking part of her crew and going in. We got 75 of them and the Reeves got the wounded 24. We left her about 5 o'clock yesterday evening. We got another contact at 7:30 last nite."

This was Dad's account of the four days of his first combat experience with the dreaded German submarine. It must have been an unsettling experience for him as well as everyone else who witnessed it and took part in fighting the submarine, burying the dead, treating wounded, rescuing crew members and performing operations to save the badly damaged USS DONNELL.

Dad states on May 3, "...... but, we got it and are we proud.". However, Lt. Cmdr. Loutrel cites in an "Action Report" dated 13 May 1944 that the sub, U-765, was sunk by a British destroyer on 6 May.

Every sailor who participated in this action has his own story and every ship has its own WAR DIARY regarding the torpedoing of the USS DONNELL. It is my effort to relate some of them which will both confirm Dad's observations and feelings and record for posterity the bravery and sacrifice the men of the destroyer escorts of CortDiv 6, TG 21.6, Convoy CU-22 exhibited and endured to help preserve the precious freedom enjoyed today by their families, communities and nation.

According to the records of the USS DONNELL, there were 25 killed and 29 wounded. On 3 May, the burial at sea commenced at 1805 and concluded at 1820, Lt. S. A. Hill, USNR, conducting the services.

The WAR DIARY of the Hopping for 3 May 1944 begins routinely.

"0001   Set clocks ahead one hour to GCT.

0630   Convoy changed course to 039 degrees T.

0700   Convoy commenced zig zag using zig zag plan #19.

0755   Ship #64 dropped astern.

0800   Position 47 degrees 29'N, 20 degrees 29W.

0811   Ordered by CTG 21.6 to drop back and determine #64's reason for straggling.

0825   #64 having repaired telemotor, rejoining at 16 knots. Ordered by CTG 21.6 to resume station.

0920   Returned to station #4.

Following action reports submitted separately cover the operations of this ship between 1000 z May 3, 1944 and 1400 z May 6, 1944."

On 10 October, 1943, Commander F. D. Giambattista, USN, a Naval Academy graduate who went on to attain the rank of Rear Admiral and died on March 3, 2001 at the age of 96, had been relieved as Commanding Officer of the Hopping by Lt. Commander L. F. Loutrel, Jr., USNR, who had served as the Executive Officer on the Hopping since its commissioning. Now, on 9 May 1944, as Commanding Officer of the Hopping, Lt. Cmd. Loutrel, as required by Naval regulations, filed a confidential report with the Commander in Chief, U. S. Fleet covering the events of May 3 through 6.

This report reveals that after the Donnell was torpedoed at 1000 hours, the Hopping made first contact with the submarine at 1035 by QCS Sonar. E. P. Crivello, 2585451A, SOM 2/C, was the seaman on duty who identified the contact.

The Commander's Narrative gives this information: "U. S. S. DONNELL (DE-56) reported sonar contact at 0954 bearing 058 degrees T., distance 2300 yards and at 0958 reported periscope dead ahead. This ship was then turning to port to assist. At 1000 the DONNELL was hit by torpedo in the stern and (according to reports of personnel later removed) this was followed a few seconds later by explosion of depth charges which had been set for anticipated attack and were blown overboard by first explosion. Ordered at 1002 by CTG 21.6 to conduct "observant" in vicinity of DONNELL and complied, dropping a life raft at 1020 near several survivors to the northeast of the DONNELL.

At 1035 sonar contact was established bearing about 300 range 1800. HOPPING was then about 2 miles southwest of DONNELL in a slow turn to starboard on course of about 320. At this time port lookout reported torpedo wake on port bow. Addition rudder and full speed were ordered steadying on course 000. FXR gear MARK 2 was in use and functioning properly. No explosion or other confirmation of torpedo was seen. Attack was commenced at 1037 with target bearing 298 degrees T., range 1500 yards, hedgehog attack was made firing pattern at 1041 on course 270 degrees T. At 1045 sonar contact reestablished and pattern fired at 1050."

Following this second attack on the submarine, there were four more attacks using two depth charge and two hedgehog attacks.

The FXR gear Mark 2 referred to was a newly developed gear which trailed behind the ship and created more noise than the ship's propeller. The FXR gear protected the ship from the newest German submarine weapon, the "Acoustic Torpedo", which would pick up a noise and direct itself to the noise for a "hit". This was the type of torpedo that hit the Donnell.

Seaman Robert O. Davidson, who was on board the Donnell, recently informed me that he had spoken by telephone in June, 2001 with one of the radar men from the Donnell who stated that the FXR gear on the Donell had been removed the day before the attack for repair because it was broken.

The Commander's Narrative continues: "At 1230 HOPPING was designated as OTC by CTG 21.6. REEVES then proceeding to assist. At 1300 REEVES directed to screen DONNELL who had reported watertight integrity forward of frame 124 and furnish medical assistance. REEVES arrived 1327 and effected transfer of medical officer and later medical supplies to DONNELL.

At 1350 when sonar contact with submarine had been lost for one hour, commenced box search. REEVES detailed to continue screening DONNELL. During the period from 1350 to 2000 conducted box search in area without contact. At about 1950, reporting HP/DP position of U-boat believed to be DONNELL's attacker as 48 degrees 10'N 20 degrees 00'W at 1722. This position plotted 30 miles bearing 060 degrees from HOPPING's location. In view of approaching darkness, and the known position of Escort Group 2 bound for the area where the U-boat was then reported, and the probability that the U-boat was then continuing on surface, the REEVES was directed to take DONNELL in tow and HOPPING set course 118 degrees T. to rejoin. This course cut diagonally across the area of previous box search. At 2010, message was received from S. O. Escort Group 2 giving (HMS SPANNING) an ETA of 2400 for his group to join in search. Reference (c) deciphered 2120 contained CinCwa's order to discontinue hunt. On the morning of 6 May, HMS WHIMBREL reported she had received a message of S. O. Escort Group 2 stating that HMS STARLING had sunk U-boat believed to be that which torpeoded DONNELL and had rescued some survivors.

Rendezvoused with DONNELL and REEVES at 2115 to find tow secured and REEVES commencing towing operation. Commenced box search around tow. Considerable difficulty was experienced due to tendency of DONNELL to yaw. A towing speed of four knots was obtained at about 2200 and as satisfactory progress was being made, HOPPING originated at 2330, reference (d), advising CinCwa of situation.

At 0125 reference (e) was broken and CinCwa's decision to scuttle DONNELL was learned. The REEVES was therefore ordered to slip tow and furnish additional strength to screen. It was noted that reference (e) had been originated prior to receipt of information on feasibility of effecting tow which had been forwarded by reference (d) and for that reason reference (f) was originated requesting confirmation. Reference (g) and (h), which were deciphered 0330 and 0515 respectively, instructed that every effort be made to save DONNELL. Reference (i) advising of detachment of HMS WHIMBREL and HMS MAGPIE was broken at about 0500 and it was calculated that these escorts should arrive at approximately 0700. It was, therefore, planned to delay transfer of DONNELL's personnel until their arrival."

The several references mentioned above were communications between the Commander, Task Group, 21.6 and The Commander in Chief, United States Fleet whether the Donnell could be saved. If it could be, it would be the first ship to be saved that had survived a German submarine torpedo attack. Another amazing fact about the Donnell is revealed in "Report of Operations" by the Commander, T.G. 21.6. "....... Upon falling of smoke and spray it could be seen that about 20-30 feet of her stern was sticking up in the air at an angle of about 70 degrees to the horizontal." This obviously made the towing by the Reeves and the Hopping far more difficult as each of them records.

USS DONNELL, DE 56

USS DONNELL, DE 56 After Torpedo Attack

"At 1303 radar contact was made on two ships bearing 035 T., 19 miles on course 160 T. Voice radio contact made and identity established as the expected escorts. They joined at 1410 with HMS WHIMBREL assuming duties as S. O. of screen and forming escorts. Tow again parted (broke) at 1552. DONNELL was at this time towing about 40 off HOPPING's port quarter, rolling 25 to 35 and with marked tendency to swing further to port if speed was increased. As a result, any seas which tended to swing HOPPING's stern to starboard put an unduly heavy strain on

Donnell with Jib Sail

the tows and eventually this strain parted the towing cable. In considering the problem it was concluded that an all chain tow (1 1/8 " dielock chain) with consequent increased catenary would be an improvement and this was undertaken. HOPPING first passing over 7 shots of chain to DONNELL to replace that lost the previous day. At 1830 DONNELL was again under tow but chain parted 45 fathoms from HOPPING's fantail at 1927. At 2115 the all chain towline was replaced and course was 101 T. steered at estimated speed of 2.5 knots. HOPPING making turns for 5 knots. This course and speed were maintained throughout the night without incident.

At 0800 5 May, weather was overcast, wind northwest, force four sea from north west, condition four. Position was 48 07'N, 18 20'W, speed of advance figured at 3.5 knots on course 010 T. with about 1 knot drift east. Reference (j) advising of assistance from tug SAMSONIA and LOCHY had been received at 0200 of the previous day. Reference (k) directing tug EMULOUS to join was received at 1100. During the morning, speed was increased slightly and with canvas passed by HMS WHIMBREL, DONNELL rigged two jibs on forecastle. With the wind on her port beam, these were a decided help in counteracting her tendencies to veer to port and resulted in towing at increased speed about 15 nearer astern. AT 1350 WHIMBREL got a sound contact, shortly classified non sub. Towing was without incident. Tug EMULOUS joined at 1755 followed at 2000 the BYMS 2047. On consultation with tug captain it was deemed feasible to use tug for transfer of personnel from DONNELL and with prospect of improved weather, indicated by clearing and rising barometer, the decision was reached by Commanding Officer of HOPPING and Commanding Officer of HMS WHIMBREL to have DONNELL continue in tow of HOPPING so as to permit use of EMULOUS's services the following morning for the transfer of injured and excess personnel.

At daybreak, 6 May 1944, weather had moderated. Wind north north west, force three swell north north west, condition two. Elected to use tug EMULOUS for transfer of injured. Course of two altered to 340 T. and speed out to 2 knots for this purpose. At 0620, EMULOUS made approach on DONNELL's port quarter, but yawing of DONNELL and some rolling of both ships soon indicated the impracticability of this maneuver for transfer of injured since it would involve possibility of damage to both REEVES and EMULOUS as well as further damage to DONNELL. At 0740, the motor whaleboat was lowered and between then and 0945, 73 men and one officer were transferred from DONNELL to HOPPING. This operation was completed with but minor injury to one man, but the need for prompt and vigorous action by men in boarding and leaving the boat made it impractical for injured personnel. It was therefore elected to attempt transfer by breeches buoy directly to the REEVES with two ships lying head on forecastles overlapping. This appreared practicable in view of DONNELL's tendency to drift astern downwind propelled by the section of fantail which was bent upwards at an acute angle. However, shortly after HOPPING slipped the tow for this purpose the wind shifted to light south west with a rapid moderation of sea, making transfer by motor whaleboat appear feasible. REEVES then lowered her boat and 25 injured, one Pharmacist Mate, and REEVES's doctor, and three passengers on board DONNELL for transfer to USS ARKANSAS, were transferred, using both motor whaleboats. The operation was completed at 1330.

Meanwhile the HMS CAMS had joined at 0610 in compliancewith reference (3). The HMS LOCHY and BYMS 2047 had been detached to Falmouth at 1000. Tug SAMSONIA secured tow to DONNELL

USS DONNELL, IX 182

at about 1340. Consequently at about 1400 HOPPING and REEVES and HMS WHIMBREL and HMS MAGPIE took departure in accordance with references (m) and (n) turning over the escort of U. S. S. DONNELL to HMS CAMS, assisted by HMS LOCHY, position was 49 23'N, 14 15"W.

    The REEVES and HOPPING set course 040 T. for Londonderry, Northern Ireland, speed 20 knots later increased to 23 knots. Enroute REEVES had sound contact which was investigated for a period of one hour and classified as doubtful. Arrived Lough Foyle sea buoy 1550 with REEVES taking pilot at once and proceeding to U. S. Naval Supply Depot, Lisaholly. Arrived 1715 and all injured personnel were transferred to U. S. Naval Dispensary, Reevaugh, Northern Ireland for treatment.

                      L. F. Loutrel, Jr.
                      Lieutenant Commander, D-V (G), USNR
                      Commanding Officer"

The USS DONNELL, DE 56, was towed safely to Scotland where its stern was cut off. The remainder of the ship was still in full operation with its valuable turbo-electric power plant, which could generate 2600 Volts, 3 phase, at half speed. Shortly after D-Day, again it was towed to Cherbourg, France to provide electric power to the city and Allied Forces. Following the war in Europe, she was towed back to Philadelphia, decommissioned and sold for scrap metal.

In an "Action Report", dated May 8, 1944, James J. Durney, Commanding Officer of the USS REEVES, DE 156 confirms the information recorded by Lt. Cmdr. Loutrel of the HOPPING but adds, in conclusion to his report: "My medical officer spent three days on the DONNELL, and from discussions with him and with survivors, I am convinced that morale on the DONNELL was exceptionally high. They had extreme difficulties, such discomfort, and very much hard work and apparently conducted themselves in a very meritorious manner. The Commanding Officer of the DONNELL was cool and at all times efficient and effective, and worked so tirelessly and so long as to have gone, in the opinion of my medical officer, past the exhaustion point. He is still carrying on at the date of this report, so far as I know, the tow not being due for several days yet. I make the definite statement that his conduct has reflected great credit on the naval service and that he should be commended accordingly."

The Captain of the USS DONNELL, DE 56 was Lieutenant Commander Gordon Street.

On May 6, according to Lt. Cmdr. Loutrel's report, between 0740 and 0945, 73 men and one officer were transferred by motor whaleboat from the Donnell to the Hopping. Also, the same day, the Reeves transferred by motor whaleboats 25 injured, one Pharmacist Mate, the Reeves' doctor and three passengers to the USS ARKANSAS for quick transport to Northern Ireland to receive medical attention. There were many challenges in making these transfers because of high winds and rough sea; but they were made without incident.

Apparently, during the transfer of the 73 men and one officer on May 6 from the Donnell to the Hopping, a surprise meeting occurred, although Dad does not refer to it in his Diary. When he was home on leave in the following month, he related to the local newspaper, **The**

Dickensonian, how he met Gerald Eugene "Gene" Culbertson in the middle of the Atlantic Ocean. They were friends before they entered the navy and, according to Gene's military record, they were sworn in together at Abingdon, VA, on January 29, 1943, left Abingdon together on February 5 and were assigned to the same basic training company at Bainbridge. The article in the newspaper tells part of their story.

The headlines read:

"IMAGINE SEEING YOU HERE!"

"Truman Fleming of the navy, home on leave last week, reports that he met an acquaintance under rather novel circumstances on his first trip out into the Atlantic on convoy duty. Survivors from a torpedoed boat were picked up by his ship and among those was Gene Culbertson of Coeburn, a brother-in-law of Mrs. Ayers Short of Clintwood. Culbertson had been thrown into the water by the explosion but was notbadly hurt. He sent a message by seaman Fleming to his wife, telling her that he was doing fine."

Eugene Culbertson and "Doc" Mason, 1944

In February, 1987 Gene Culbertson was interviewed at length by the same local paper where it gave his account of the same incident: "Culbertson left New York aboard a destroyer escort on April 23, 1944. The ship, on which he served as a gunner, was hit by torpedo fire in the Bay of Biscayne, 800 miles off the coast of France. Twenty nine men lost their lives in the attack. Culbertson suffered a broken knee and back injuries. He was picked up by the destroyer Hopping. Culberson recalls, "To my surprise, one of the first men I saw on the Hopping was former Dickenson County Sheriff Truman Fleming. I was never so happy to see anyone.

Culbertson was taken to a convalescent hospital in Crevaugh, Ireland. He was later transferred to a hospital in Oban, Scotland where he spent four months. From there he was returned to the states for further medical treatment and was given a medical discharge Jan. 3, 1945."

What a coincidence and a surprise this meeting must have been for both! Since they knew each other before their navy days, drafted the same day, sworn in the same day, left on the same train for basic training, went through the same basic training company together, went to New York together and assigned to "sister" ships and experienced this close encounter. There's more to their story which the Diary will tell on the next trip from New York to Londonderry.

The Diary continues as Dad completes his first trans-Atlantic crossing on the Hopping and what a trip it must have been for the first time at sea, participating in a deadly engagement with the enemy and visiting a foreign country!

Sunday, May 7 "This morning at 9:30 I saw land of the Irish Free State. Something I never thought of, the grass is green and so are the trees. Its summer here but a very cool climate. A funny world over here. It's black out here all the time. Doesn't get dark until about 11 at nite and only about 4 hours. It is 11:10 now and at home it's 5:10. The clock went up last nite again. What is home like now? I am wondering."

Monday, May 8 "Registered at the Red Cross Service Club. I had liberty today in Londonderry, Ireland. I was around over the town quite a bit. It is nothing like the States. I came back at 12 o'clock. It just was dark at midnite. Gets day lite at 5:30. It's all horse and wagon. Autos drive on the left of the road and steer the car on the right side. Sure is funny to me. It is cold here, now. But it's summer for the Irish. Always Remember."

Tuesday, May 9 "Today we painted the passage ways. I hear we are leaving tomorrow. Well, I hope so. Give me the U. S. It has rained all day and still raining. It is 6:20 now and I am hitting my sack, making ready for a rough ride."

Wednesday, May 10 "This morning at 10 o'clock we left Londonderry headed back for the States. The first I saw of the convoy was at 3 o'clock this evening. It is awful rough. Last nite at 11:30 we had an air raid but didn't amount to much. It is 8 o'clock now."

Thursday, May 11 "This morning I was on watch from 4-8. It was very windy and cold. This evening I was on from 4-6. Tonite I will be on from 12-4. I just ate chow, spagetti & hamburger rolls. Very good. I am thinking what you all are doing & I want to see you all. Hope how soon I get back to N. Y. so I can go home on 72 hr. leave to see all of you."

Friday, May 12 "Just another day at sea. The same old routine - patrolling- along pretty rough and plenty of water. A drill at 3 o'clock. Meat balls for supper and cake."

Saturday, May 13 "A drill at 3:30, then off until six. A contact at 7 miles away. Stay alert. And how are all the folks back home. Stew for supper and very good, too. On watch from 6-8. Clocks went back at seven."

Sunday, May 14 "On watch from 4-8. I saw the sun over the horizon and thought of Mother's Day. 5:30 here and 3:30 at home. We will probably get in N. Y. Friday or Sat., if no bad luck. Today is a holiday routine for Mother's Day. Love to all. W. T. F."

Sunday, May 14 "Mother's Day. 8 P.M. Sunday nite. At 4 o'clock this evening we had sailed 5519 miles from N. Y. We were 1513 mi. from Londonderry, Ireland. Only five days out. We should get in N. Y. Fri. or Sat. 'Greetings to Mother' When this war is over and I am at home telling my family all about the different countries and waters, I only hope I can remember all the things that happened & how I felt & things looked, for I sure have seen some mighty sad & horrible days in the Navy so far, especially in the North Atlantic. My love for Violet & kids & mama can never be questioned anymore. <u>Truman.</u>"

Monday, May 15 "Today has been beautiful. The sun has been hot. I was on watch from 12-4 today. At 2:15 P. M. today I was thinking what C. B. & Bill were doing. It was 11:15 there. I just imagined they were feeding their team, fixing for dinner. Only wish I knew. Now it is 7:25 & 4:25 there & what are you all doing. I wonder a lot."

Tuesday, May 16 "Today was a pretty day. I slept from 12:30 until 3 o'clock. We had G. Q. At 3:30. I am trying hard for an extra 48 hr. on my leave. I sure do feel good now we are out of enemy waters. We are about 1250 or 1300 miles from New York. I was on watch from 8-12 today. I bought a box of candy to bring you. What is it worth? Ho Ho."

Wednesday, May 17 "This morning at 8 o'clock we were 940 miles out of N. Y. We sure had some fun today firing all guns on the ship. It sure was a roar for about 45 minutes. The 1 point 1 gun fired 281 rounds in 55 seconds. Guns have roared all day from the convoy. "Just drills." I have been writing today. I bought you a box of candy yesterday."

Thursday, May 18 "Today has been very rough. I was on watch from 12-4. We were lying in the gun mount when all at once a wave spray came over and really gave me a salt bath, but the sun was hot & soon dried me but left the salt all over me. Ho Ho."

Friday, May 19 "Today was cool but the water was lots calmer. The convoy is leaving us two & three ships at a time every day or two. We were 500 miles out of N. Y. this morning at 8 o'clock. Will pull in around 3 or 4 tomorrow."

The ship's WAR DIARY states that on 18 May, tankers MILL SPRING and KENYON were detached for Curacao; 19 May, HMS RULER, M/V ROSEBUD and STK BUNKER HILL were detached for Hampton Roads under escort of USS D. T. GRIFFIN and 20 May, STK FORT BRIDGER detached for Wilmington, Delaware. Also, the Hopping moored at 2020 alongside USS CHARLES LAWRENCE at Pier K Navy Yard, New York to commence 10 days availability.

Saturday, May 20 "At 8 o'clock this morning we were 80 mi. from N. Y. I saw land of the U. S. at 11:30 today. Sure looked good. Unloaded ammunition after noon. Pulled in Brooklyn, N. Y. at 8:15 tonite. Got pay & went out to call Virgil. I called at 10 o'clock tonite. Now all my mail comes."

The ship's log states the following for this date: "1930 Underway having unloaded all ammunition to Fort Lafayette lighter. 2020 Moored alongside USS Charles Lawrence at Pier K Navy Yard, New York to commence 10 days availability."

Sunday, May 21 "I am lying around today, resting up. Will leave here next Thursday, so they say, on my 96 hr. leave. I will write some today.

All my mail last nite was company and thanks for the prayers. I sure needed them from May 3 to 8."

Monday, May 22 "Today has been pretty hot here. We are just working trying to pass off time until Thursday noon."

Tuesday, May 23 "Still working, making the ship look good. Painting the rust and getting ready for my leave."

Wednesday, May 24 "Still painting the ship. I went to the dentist at 7:30 this morning. Came back at noon. Epling came back aboard today at 3 o'clock. Boy, we both were please, too! It is 9:30 P. M. now."

Thursday, May 25 "At noon today I left for my 96 hr. leave. Left N. Y. At 1:30 P. M. Arrived at Wash., D. C. at 4:20 P. M. Left Wash. At 11:50. It is 8 o'clock A. M."

Friday, May 26 "I arrived in Abingdon this morning at 10 o'clock. Was in Clintwood at 12 noon. Sure was glad to see my family and Mama."

Saturday, May 27 "We ate dinner with Maggie & Fred today. Took pictures this evening and went to church. I sure did enjoy myself at service. Hope I'll get back again."

This ends the first ocean voyage for Dad and the sixth convoy Atlantic crossing for the USS HOPPING. It took 15 days to make the trip from New York to Londonderry because of the delayed action involving the USS DONNELL. They were there 2 days and the return trip took 11 days. The events that happened during this time were indelibly etched in the minds of those who lived through them and those with whom they shared them. Even at my young age, I still remember Dad telling us briefly about the ship being torpedoed, although I do not remember the names or details as described in his Diary or the HOPPING's WAR DIARY but I can remember him describing the green grass of Ireland which seemed so beautiful to me at the time and it not getting dark until 11:00 pm and daylight by 4:00 am which was really strange to my young and inexperienced mind. It is an appropriate ending, too, being at home with his family which he missed so much as his Diary reveals.

Yet, there were more miles to travel, oceans to cross, battles to fight and new experiences to gain before he returned home for good.

Chapter Seven

Rediscovery of the Diary and More From A Survivor Of The USS DONNELL

Mother had mentioned to her children from time to time that Dad kept a diary during his time in the navy but she never offered to share it with us during the years after his death in 1958.

In the summer of 1996 my three sisters came to visit her for a few days where she still lived on the same small farm where she and dad started in 1930. During the visit my wife and I joined them at mother's house to enjoy the family time and to reminisce about the good times our family had over the years. Someone mentioned the Diary and Mother said she had kept it in a safe place all these years and would like to share it with us now. She retrieved the Diary from a bedroom locked chest drawer and then led us to his navy issued trunk where we found several pictures of his time in the navy. It was then that we discovered he had kept it in two separate journals, the Hartford Fire Insurance Company 1944 Yearbook and a small pocket sized notebook. We spent the next several hours reading the Diary, discussing it with Mother and looking at the pictures.

It was a special time for all of us, especially Mother, because she was so proud of him for serving his country and, of course, it brought back many memories of the "tough times" she endured in his absence. My sister, Fern, asked Mother if she could take the diaries and make copies for each of her siblings so we could have it to pass to our children and Mother agreed. Fern made copies, sent one to each of us and returned the originals to Mother.

Mother died in November, 1999 at the age of 88. Being one of the co-executors of her estate, I had the responsibility of separating and dispensing her personal belongings. During this process I came across the small pocket sized journal and pictures but the Hartford Yearbook was missing and has not yet been located. Since I had a complete copy of both, I began to consider writing an account, in so far as I would be able, to preserve this part of our family's history for future generations.

My search for supporting information began very slowly. At first I visited a local library to see whatever information might be available regarding the USS HOPPING and found a brief history of the ship in "The Dictionary of American Naval Fighting Ships". After that I had very limited resources except for my older brothers who, after 55years, had sketchy recollections of events and, of course, Dad's shipmates if only I could locate any of them who might still be living! The challenge now was to locate the shipmates. But where to begin?

The search took about nine months during which time I visited libraries, read World War II accounts in books, magazines, newspapers and kept a vigilant lookout for any information that might lead me to the USS HOPPING shipmates.

About September, 2000 while reading the **Bristol Herald Courier**, a local newspaper in Bristol, VA, I came across an article regarding a local chapter of the Destroyer Escort Sailor's Association (DESA) with a name and phone number of a person to call if anyone had any questions. Of course I had questions! I called James Klepper, introduced myself and told him that I was seeking information regarding anyone related to the destroyer, USS HOPPING. Mr. Klepper knew of the Hopping and that the shipmates had had recent reunions. He referred me to the national organization of DESA in Deland, Florida.

After several searches and a few days, the secretary of DESA was able to provide me with a list of four names and addresses of men who had served on the Hopping. With great anticipation of locating one of Dad's shipmates and the possibility of finding one who actually remembered him, I wrote letters to each one. Three of the letters were returned by the postal service but one was answered!!

Anderson F. Johnson of Deltaville, VA, who went aboard the Hopping in October, 1945 responded with a list of the shipmates from a recent reunion that included addresses and some phone numbers. Immediately I began calling. After several unsuccessful attempts, a valuable contact was made with Willis "Bill" C. Dailey in Oneonta, NY. He led me to Charles "Chuck" J. Buice in Winston-Salem, NC who referred me to Robert "Shorty" M. Miller in Phoenix, AZ who led me to Alfred "Al" Vilardi in Sebastian, FL who was the coordinator of the last reunion as well as the upcoming reunion. Each of these men has been an invaluable and willing resource in sharing his recollections and information regarding the USS HOPPING.

As I began to converse by telephone with these men and others who served on the destroyer escorts in World War II and continued my reading about the ships and their crews, I began to develop a deep respect for what they did in service of their country. All of this prompted me to take the diary Dad had left and prepare it for my family, the shipmates of the Hopping, the destroyer escort sailors and anyone else who might be interested in reading a small capsule of Dad's experiences, a brief history of a destroyer, her crew and events that were a part of one of the most critical times in world history.

During my quest for information regarding the Hopping, as I mentioned before, James Klepper of Mount Carmel, TN was the first contact. He is the CEO of the Tri-State Chapter of DESA having served on the USS FARQUHAR, DE 139 in World War II. Mr. Klepper has been a great resource of information regarding the destroyers. It was through him that I met Robert "Rob" O. Davidson of Rogersville, TN who was on the USS DONNELL, DE 56 when it was torpedoed on May 3, 1944. To me, this was a most fortunate opportunity because I could actually talk with a survivor of the USS DONNELL!!

I called Rob to inquire if I could visit him to talk about his experiences on the Donnell. He readily agreed but hastily added that he doubted if he could be of any help since he probably has forgotten most of it. That was fine with me because I was excited to meet and talk with a man who had survived the horrifying experience of having his ship torpedoed by a German submarine in the frigid North Atlantic. We set the date and time.

When I drove into his driveway, I was met by one of the most humble, enthusiastic, jolly and wonderful men I have ever met. After exchanging a few words of greeting and welcoming, he escorted me into his house and introduced me to his equally lovely wife, Ina. Their home was very comfortable, showing evident signs of a happy and successful life together.

I began the interview by sharing some quotes from the Diary of May 3. Rob began to remember things clearly. He shared some pictures of the Donnell and related how he was asleep in his bunk when the torpedo hit.

S 2/C Robert O. Davidson

He remembered the explosion but doesn't remember anything else until he awoke several feet under water with a blanket wrapped around his feet. He began kicking to get the blanket off his feet in order to get to the surface so he could breath. He had been blown from his bunk off the ship and into the water. One of the pictures shows how the deck buckled by the explosion and the officers later surmised that the only way he escaped was by being blown through the buckled hole in the deck. He spent over 2 hours in the water holding to a life preserver that a rescuer had thrown him. When he was finally pulled from the water, his hands had to be pried from the preserver because he was so cold. They put him on a stretcher and hoisted him back on board the Donnell. He was conscious of all activity around him and said he was very uneasy because he was informed that the German sub was still in the area and the ship was a "sitting duck" for another attack. He was treated for multiple contusions and spent the first night on a stretcher on the second deck. He remembered Taps being played as the deceased were buried at sea. The burial ceremonies were still fresh in his mind even after these 56 years because as he said, "Except for the grace of God, I could have been one of them."

Donnell's Buckled Deck

Officer in Passageway

Davidson's Rescue

During our conversation, Rob related one of the most interesting personal experiences I could have ever imagined. When he arrived back on board the Donnell, the medics and doctors were treating the wounded and he noticed a certain seaman being treated for his wounds. Upon closer observation he noticed the seaman had had his skull blown off except the skin of his forehead which was still attached and a medic holding his skull in his hand with the seaman's brain exposed. Rob said the wounded man was conscious and alert and he observed that when the wounded seaman spoke he could see his brain move!

The medics reattached his skull and the seaman seemed to be alert when he last saw him on board the Donnell. This is not the end of the story! Rob was transferred to the USS ARKANSAS and hurried to Ireland for further treatment along with others who had been wounded. He met the seaman in the hospital in Ireland and he was recovering! Then Rob was later transferred back to St. Albans Hospital in New York where he again met the same seaman. The seaman told him the doctors had inserted a steel plate and he expected to fully recover.

Rob further related that he had read a newspaper story within the past 5-10 years about the seaman recounting his story. Rob said he had forgotten the man's name but that he lived somewhere in New England. I had earlier obtained a copy of the 29 wounded men on the Donnell and found John E. Wallace, S 2/C, who was listed in the ship's log with a "Diag. Fracture Compound Skull" but was, at the time, unable to confirm him as the wounded seaman. What an incredible story!

In November, 2004, while on a Caribbean reunion cruise with shipmates from the Hopping, Donnell and Reeves, Howard Tiedemann, who was on the Donnell when it was hit, not only confirmed the story of John E. Wallace's wound and recovery but also furnished pictures as positive proof. I began to more fully understand why many combat veterans would prefer not to talk about their experiences to those of us who have lived such sheltered lives.

The shipmates of the USS DONNELL, DE 56 met in Chicago in 1997 for a reunion. Rob was reunited with a friend who shared the tragic events on May 3, 1944 with him. It was Ernest E. Steele, Jr. from Lebanon, PA. As Rob related the story, he and Ernest were the only two survivors who were blown into the sea and Ernest was blown over the ship's mast on his mattress! The men on the Hopping confirmed that they saw a man blown over the mast on his mattress. The war produced many incredible stories and the aforementioned are certainly among them. Still these men never sought recognition.

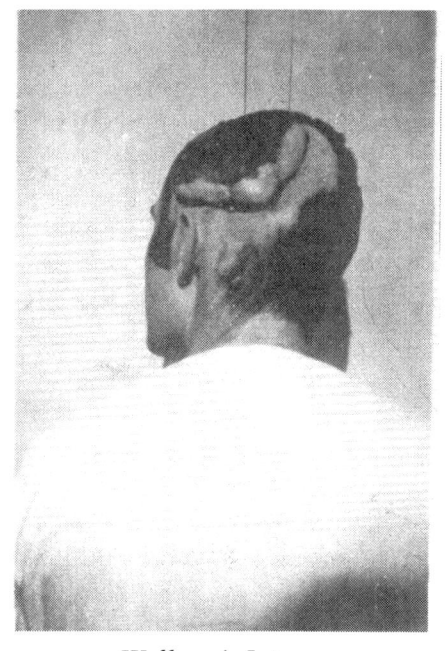

Wallace's Injury   *Wallace's Recovery*

Davidsons and Steeles, Chicago Reunion, 1997

Donnell Survivors, Chicago Reunion, 1997

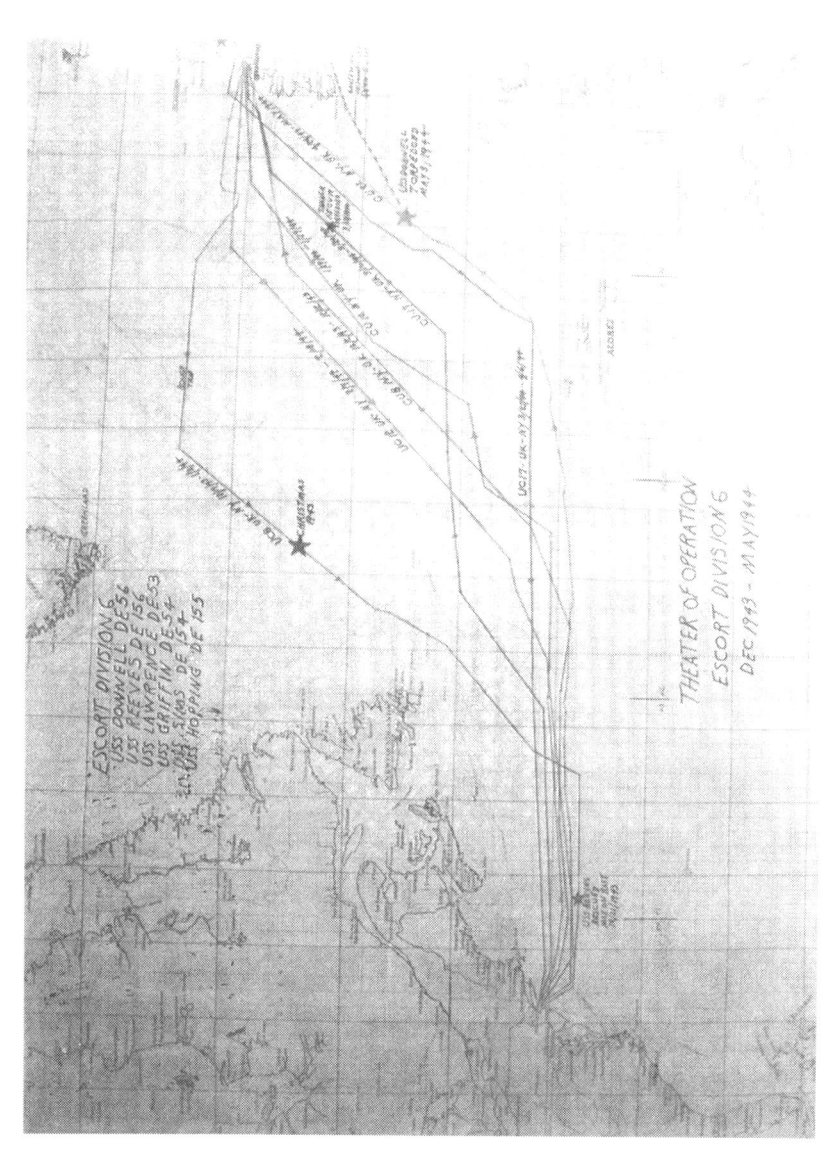

*Atlantic Theater of Operation
Escort Division 6,
Dec. 1943 - May 1944*

Chapter Eight

"Make The Best Out Of Life You Can"

After the interlude of the previous chapter, the story, as related in the Diary, continues with a brief leave for Dad following his first trans-Atlantic voyage.

As recorded earlier, his ship moored at Pier K Navy Yard, New York on May 20 at 2020 hours. He was granted a 96 hour leave on Thursday May 25 and arrived home the next day at 10:00 a. m. In order to get back to his ship on time he had to leave home Sunday morning to return to Abingdon to catch the train back to New York. There was no car in our family during his absence probably because gas was strictly rationed and automobiles were restricted to those who had jobs; however, relatives and friends were always willing to provide him transportation to and from Abingdon when he came home on leave and the family walked the 1 ½ miles to town when we needed groceries. In fact, we developed an income for the family by carrying milk, eggs, butter, chickens and other farm products to "customers" in town and purchased our food staples such as flour, meal, sugar, etc. with the ration stamps. We were fortunate to live on a farm and produce most of our food including meats, vegetables, fruits and dairy products. It is my clear recollection that during this period family, friends and neighbors were very caring and helpful. There was a strong bonding among the people in our community to take care of each other. We did not have government agencies to provide any assistance. This created a very strong family, community and national unit and we were blessed by that. It now seems very unlike today when many people depend upon our government and abdicate their responsibility.

WWII Ration Stamps

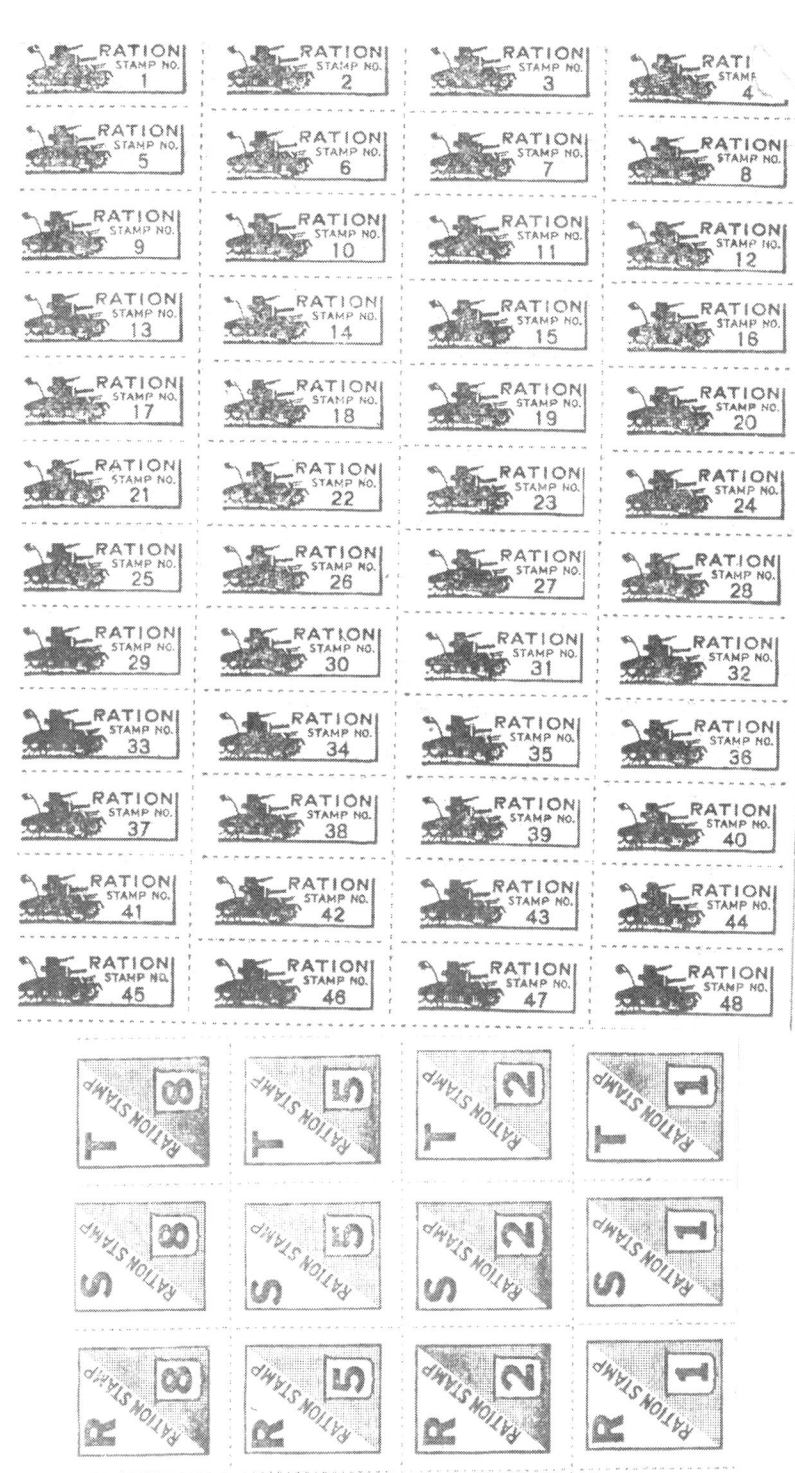

WWII Ration Stamps

The Diary resumes where he left off on Saturday, May 27.

Sunday, May 28 "This morning was the saddest Sunday I ever saw in my life when I left home to return. I thought I couldn't stand it at all. Maybe I'll come home some day to stay. I cried all day & nite and prayed, too."

Monday, May 29 "I got in Brooklyn this morn. at 2 o'clock. Got a bed at the Y. M. C. A. and slept till 10. Then came to the ship at 11:20, had chow and went on watch. It is 7:15 now and don't seem like I can stand to live. We are leaving Wednesday morning."

Tuesday, May 30 "We turned to until 11 and had liberty after noon. I went out in town and came back at 6 o'clock."

Wednesday, May 31 "We were off this morning at 8 o'clock and went out and loaded ammunition. It took us until 9:30 to finish loading and boy were we tired. Then out to sea."

Thursday, June 1 "We headed up at Long Island today. Our sound gear is no good. We fished some, too. Caught some blow fish. We will be underway tomorrow morning at 6:30 a. m. It is 6:15 now p. m. Has been raining some today."

Friday, June 2 "We were at Casio Bay today. The sun is hot but it was foggy this morning. The day is pretty. I got sunburned today. Had fish for dinner."

Saturday, June 3 "Today was pretty until about three. We pulled in at Long Island again. Our movies tonite were Roy Rogers & Smiley Burnett in "Idaho". Hope all is well at home. I've wondered all day."

Sunday, June 4 "We had firing today at 5:30 p. m. I saw a big shark. We shot several times at it and got one. We anchored at 6 o'clock and had a swimming party. Holiday routine this afternoon."

Another brief article appeared in the local newspaper, **The Dickensonian**, on June 4 and shows some light humor on Dad's part as well as the owner and editor of the paper. It reads: "Truman Fleming, former political stalwart in this county is now a crewman aboard a Destroyer Escort somewhere in the Atlantic. He writes that he is a good

Baptist and that he believes in immersion, but not quite so dadburned often. He was recently home on furlough."

Monday, June 5 "Fired torpedoes today and set sail for N. Y. tonite at 8 o'clock."

Tuesday, June 6 "We arrived in N. Y. at 11 today. Starboard had liberty."

A special note was inserted in the Diary at this point. It apparently was a note Dad had mailed to Mother and he entered it in the Diary as a reminder of their upcoming anniversary on June 23.

It reads: "June 7, 44

Dear,

This is to remind you of fourteen years back.

I am leaving tomorrow morning. So make the best out of life you can.

Lovingly yours,

Truman"

Wednesday, June 7 "I had liberty from 12 to 12. Went to Coney Island and made the record and mailed it home. Guess it will please the kids or I hope so. Came in at 11 o'clock."

Thursday, June 8 "Off this morning at 8:30. Don't know where to, for certain. Violet, I am just like I left you except a little bit heavier. Ho! Ho! And will be when you see me again."

Friday, June 9 "Today finds us something like 5 or 600 miles out from New York. They changed me from the 1.1 to the K. Guns. On continual watch. We heard that there were two subs in this vicinity but we have not contacted yet. It has been awful pretty so far."

Saturday, June 10 "Today has been beautiful. The water is as blue as the sky....this notes deep water and pretty weather. A convoy one day ahead of us lost one tanker and another one got hit. It went back to N. Y. We are making 14 knots. Hope to land safe."

Sunday, June 11 "I was on watch from 8 - 12 this morning. I wondered what you were doing at 7 and at 9 and again a 5 & 6 and at 7 tonite. I am just off watch. I have washed, brushed my teeth and now I will hit my sack until 3:30 in the morning. I can see you & the kids & mom milking & feeding. I am about 1/3 of the way across now. 'Good nite to all'."

Monday, June 12 "Today has been rough. It has rained all day until about 3:30. We refueled about 7 o'clock tonite. Getting ready for attacks. Guess we will have plenty trouble from here on. We are five and one half days from N. Y."

Tuesday, June 13 "I have been serving life line this morning. I go on watch at 12. It is still pretty rough out here. We are about half way now. About tomorrow or next day we will be about where the Donnell was hit so it is tough going from here on. Hope we get through OK so I can see you all again."

Wednesday, June 14 "Today has been very nice. Last nite 3 torpedo boats were reported 150 miles out headed this way & plenty subs are marked up at the Chart House. We are looking for air and U. Boat attacks any time. We are about 4 days from Ireland. 4:25 now."

Thursday, June 15 "Today has been cloudy and misting rain but the water has been pretty calm. We all are getting plenty contacts on fish but good luck so far about subs. Well, I think an awful lot about you all but what good does it do. Just shows I would love to be home."

Dad's above statement, "We all are getting plenty contacts on fish but good luck so far about subs.", is confirmed by an entry in the Hopping's WAR DIARY for June 15: *"1627 Convoy executed emergency left turn after sound contacts by DT Griffin and C. Lawrence resuming course at 1631 when contacts classified non-sub. Numerous sonar contacts on fish followed throughout afternoon."*

Several other entries in the Hopping's log during the days of June 14 - 18 referenced sonar contacts resulting in schools of fish instead of submarines. This type of sonar activity must have been very unsettling to the officers and crew on board all the ships in the convoy. They knew they were in dangerous waters and the submarines were difficult to detect and identify before their devastating attacks.

Friday, June 16 "Today has been nice. It is 5:50 now and the sun sure is coming down. Still no subs. Field day today. Captain's inspection just finished. We are about 1000 miles from Ireland. Just had chow and it was a big steak. Boy, fish are plentiful out here now. It is 2 p.m. at home but 6 here."

Saturday, June 17 "It has been awful cold today. We hit a wolf pack. The Cates & Griffin got one - they say at 1:30. We are 700 miles from Ireland. It is awful foggy and plenty white caps. A good time for subs now. We are close to England today. They dropped several 12,000 lbs. bombs. We heard the guns in battle. I was eating chow today at noon when we heard the guns popping in France. A man broadcasted that dead Germans were found in piles. And this morning you should of heard our charges going off on subs. Boy, have we thinned them out in this area?"

At this point, the Hopping and convoy were in the English Channel and close enough to hear the battle raging in Europe. D-Day had begun on June 6 and was continuing on this date. What could have been the feelings he experienced that day?

Sunday, June 18 "We dropped 12 charges this morning at 8:30. It is some warmer now. I was on watch from 4-6. At 4:30 I sat and studied, well, it's 12:30 at home. What can they all be doing? I am one day from Ireland & land. Well, I have studied Cumberland Mt. from the Blue Head flats to Pine Mt. about all my hunting, etc. I wrote letters tonite, V., mom, Fred and Claudia. To England and then to Ireland. 8:30 now. I must hit my sack. P. S. Would this be my nite, if I were home? Ho, Ho."

This duty was unusual for the Hopping since it was delivering a convoy of ships directly to the English Channel instead of Lisahally, N.I. I found the explanation in the book, **The Two-Ocean War** by Samuel Eliot Morison, p 408. "On D-day plus 12, June 18, everything in both sectors was "all tickety-boo," to use a favorite phrase of Field Marshall Montgomery for describing military perfection. By the end of that day, 314,514 troops, 41,000 vehicles and 116,000 tons of supplies had been landed over the American beaches; 314,547 troops, 54,000 vehicles and 102,000 tons of supplies over the British beaches. Then, Nature intervened with the worst June storm in forty years."

The Hopping had participated in landing this massive number of troops, vehicles and supplies at the Omaha beaches in preparation of the allied forces liberating Cherbourg, France, which was a critical seaport for the continuation of the defeat of Germany. It left Omaha beaches before the devastating storm hit and proceeded to Lisahally to join another convoy returning to New York.

Monday, June 19 "Belfast at 9 o'clock and on to Londonderry. At 12 today we singled up to take the convoy to England. The other DE's left us at 3 o'clock. We will get back to Londonderry tomorrow morning. I haven't seen land yet - should about midnite tonite. Hope to get home around the 10th of July. We arrived without any trouble at all."

Tuesday, June 20 "We went to Belfast yesterday. Left at 4 and got back here this morning at 7:30. About 9 last nite I saw land in Belfast then went to bed and woke up this morning in Ireland. 13 days this time over. Gene (*Culbertson, wounded in the attack on the Donnell*) has just left. He has been down to see me. It is 9:15 p.m. now and the sun is about three hours high. It gets dark at 1:15 and day at 5. Hope we leave here soon. I see bombers coming back in formation from homing mission every little bit."

Wednesday, June 21 "I was on liberty today from 1 to 12 tonite. I went up to see Culbertson and Crisp at Buck Hill. They are getting along fine but would like to come back to the States. I ate chow with them and talked a long time with them. Well, I was married 14 years ago next Friday and I sure am proud of you, 'Sweetheart', Love."

Bethel E. Crisp referred to above was inducted at Abingdon, VA. on January 29, 1944 with Dad, Culbertson, and Epling. Crisp is listed with the Donnell wounded and was transferred to the Hopping on May 6 along with Culbertson and the others to be transported to Londonderry for treatment of their wounds. Apparently being from the same geo-

*Londonderry, 1944Londonderry, 2004*graphic area afforded them the opportunity to establish a common bond.It is quiet possible that Crisp also was in the same basic training company at Bainbridge, MD. In addition, my research revealed that Jacob Morgan Deel, Carlos Albert Deskins and Grover Madison Dooley served onthe USS HOPPING at the same time and were all inducted at Abingdon, VA.

Londonderry, 1944

Londonderry, 2004

73

Londonderry, 1944

Londonderry, 2004

Thursday, June 22 "Today is a little cloudy but very nice for Londonderry, Ireland. I went out to buy some souvenirs to bring home. Crisp came down and had supper with me. Culbertson ate dinner with me and gave me his Purple Heart to take back to his wife. It is pretty. They are awful lonesome. I am too."

Gene Culbertson was transferred from Londonderry on June 30 to a hospital in Boston and to other hospitals until he was discharged at the Naval Hospital, Fort Eustis, Va. on January 3, 1945. He lived in Dickenson County the rest of his life and died December 7, 1995. I visited his daughter, Sue Thompson, at her home where she showed me the Purple Heart her father had kept throughout the years.

Friday, June 23 "I have thought every hour today of what happened 14 yrs. ago about 6 o'clock. Though we are many miles apart, I must say I love that day and this one too. I think of you every minute, if possible, and love you more too. I bought you, mom & sis something to remember our 14th anniversary by. It is now 9 o'clock here and 3 there. We are leaving tomorrow, so good bye until I see you, 'Dearest One'. Love."

Saturday, June 24 "We left Ireland this morning at 6 o'clock for the States, that was 12 midnite at home. I was thinking of Charles Burns' birthday just about the time he was born. The sea is plenty rough up here ao far north as this. I heard we were going to Cherbourg, France next time. It is 8 now. I will hit my sack. Good Nite."

Sunday, June 25 "It has been rough today. We had a holiday routine all day and believe me I slept from 8:30 until 12 & from 12:30 until 3:30. Now it is 6:15 and I will sleep until 12 tonite. Two days out of Ireland. We should get in the 4th or 5th of July. Hope all is well at home. It is 1:15 there."

Monday, June 26 "6 o'clock now and still rough. I just ate. We are in red torpedo junction now and anything could happen. I will be on watch from 8-12 tonite. Had cookies & pineapples for chow. Hope to see you all soon. I am trying for a leave."

Tuesday, June 27 "It has been awfully rough today. So bad we had to stand watch inside because waves are coming clean over top. You have to hold just to stand up. We should get in around the 5th of July. They say we only get 48 hrs. this time. If so, I'll call soon as I get in N. Y."

The last sentence in the above entry is interesting because it is the first reference to making a telephone call. I cannot establish when we got our first home telephone installed but it was in the early 1940's and we had the first one in our small community. (My daughter still has the wooden box phone with most of the "works" in tact.) There were other phones on the same party line, too. I can remember Mother listening to make sure someone else was not on the line before she would make a call. Also, one of the phones was at Joe Baker's Store which was a small general store just outside the town limits on the road to our house about one mile away. When Mother was out of the house, my older brothers would "ring up" the store and ask: "Do you have Prince Albert in the can?" (A popular roll-your-own tobacco in a metal can.) When Joe would answer "Yes", they would say: "You'd better let him out before he smothers." This was very funny and entertaining to my brothers and me but I'm sure not to Joe Baker.

Wednesday, June 28 "It is still rough out here and subs are in this area. We will be half way tomorrow sometime - from Ireland. I hope I get to see you all. Several planes will make contact with us tonite after midnite sometime."

Thursday, June 29 "I heard that we would be in the 4th. If so, I will get to see you soon. It is still rough going but we are making it fine. Several of the boys are awfully sea sick. I am yet a lucky guy about sea sick. Well, some day I'll join in with you all for a long talk and stay. Ho! Best Wishes tonite."

Friday, June 30 "I asked Mr. Miller, 1st Lt., this evening for a special leave and he took it up with the Exec. & Capt. for me. It was ok! The Capt. told him to take me to the Red Cross as soon as we get in and get me out of here. Said I must have a draft board at my home that didn't like me. They sure treated me nice. 'But a man should use his tongue at the right time in the right way.' I sure was surprised when the Lt. & Capt. & Exec. called to my attention about 1:30 today that I should be home and not in here, with the family I had. I sure will not forget this day and my officers for that." *(Lt.Cmdr. Louis F. Loutrel, Jr., Captain; Lt. Willard J. McNulty, Executive Officer and 1st Lt. R. C. Miller)*

Saturday, July 1 "It is nice and very calm today. I was on watch from 4-8 this morning. Watched the beautiful sunrise. About 1,000 miles from land now. Get in on the 4th. We are holding field day today. Probably a holiday routine tomorrow. A rain cloud is rising in the West horizon."

Sunday, July 2 "We have had a holiday routine today. It's 6 o'clock and I just ate chow - pears, pickles, pork & beans, horse meat, potato salad and cocoa. A plane just has met us to patrol in. I'm all packed & ready to start soon as I get in docks."

Monday, July 3 "Today was nice except a bit rough. Should get in tomorrow."

Tuesday, July 4 "I left today at 12 noon and got in at 7:30 this morn. Left Washington at 6:35; got in Lynchburg at 11:30; left at 3:30; got in Bluefield (*WVa*) at 8:30; home at 2:30."

Wednesday, July 5 "Arrived home at 2:30 today with a surprise to all!"

Thursday, July 6 "I was in town today and met several friends. Melvin (*Fleming, great uncle, for whom Dad had great respect.*) came down and talked until dark with me."

Friday, July 7 "It has rained all day. I have been getting ahead on my sleeping. It is 9:15 now and seems funny hearing the frogs & chickens & calves and no planes or guns or seeing the waves break over as they do at sea."

Saturday, July 8 "Went to town and then up to see Dan (*father-in-law*). He is pretty bad sick - weighs 218 lbs."

Sunday, July 9 "Went to Grandma's & back to see Dan. Had supper with them."

When he refers to "Grandma's" in the above entry, this is his grandmother, Grandma Morgan in Jenkins, Ky. I can vaguely remember making the trip in a crowded car on a very hot day over the crooked road from Clintwood to Jenkins. In the car was Dad, Mother, Grandma Minerva Morgan Fleming and all six of us children. I usually got car sick and this trip was no exception. Grandma Morgan was about 75 years old at the time. She also was a full blooded Cherokee Indian. Several aunts, uncles and cousins came to visit her that day in order to see Dad and get a first hand report of his navy experiences.

Monday, July 10 "I was in town to see about my papers. Got them fixed. All but the Board."

Tuesday, July 11 "Picked berries until 1:00 o'clock today. Got enough to make 29 quarts of jam."

I do remember this day! It was my 10th birthday! I remember going with the entire family to pick the berries and I had to pick, too. Everyone was expected to help out to prepare food for the coming winter. When we returned we had to prepare the fire for a large wash tub in which the cans were placed to be washed. We had to prepare the berries for Mom and Dad to cook before they were placed in the jars. Mom and Dad were the overseers to make sure everything was done properly. When all was finished the cans were put in a large stone cellar along with over 300 other canned fruits, vegetables and meats for our consumption during the coming winter months.

These were good days because Dad was safely home even though only for a short while.

Wednesday, July 12 "Picked berries this morning. We got about 7 gals. Went up to Mr. Stanley's (*Lee Stanley, a close friend*) and had supper. We had a swell time. Came back and went up to Earl Mullins' (*Pastor of Flemingtown Freewill Baptist Church*) for prayer meeting."

Thursday, July 13 "It is raining this morning."

Friday, July 14 "I went up today and filled out my papers. Got back at 8:30 P.M. Mom, Fred, Maggie were up with me until 11:30. Claudia was up. Left at 6 for home. It has been hot here today."

Saturday, July 15 "Violet brought me to Coeburn. Left there at 7:30 and arrived in Abingdon at 10 A.M. Got a shave, hair cut & shampoo & shoe shine. Am here in the station writing. Hope to get a telegram when I get to N.Y. It is 11:10 now and train is due at 11:50. I don't have to buy a ticket at all. I'll use the one I have from Bluefield."

Sunday, July 16 "Arrived in Brooklyn this morning at 3 o'clock. Went to bed at Y.M.C.A. Got up at 8 and went down to receiving station, checked in and went to ship at noon. Mr. Miller called Red Cross but they were out. I will go up to Red Cross in the morning at eight."

Monday, July 17 "Reveille at 6:30. Chow at 7. Muster at quarters at 8. Mr. Miller called me out to go to meet with Mrs. Hopping. Caught bus and went up. Mrs. Hopping brought me back to ship. I had chow at 12 and went on watch from 12-4. I was called at 6 to leave on a 30 day leave. Left at 8 o'clock. Arrived in Washington at 12.25. Went to servicemen's center. Got me a bunk."

Tuesday, July 18 "Up at 7 this morning. Got breakfast at cafe and left at 8:05. Arrived in Abingdon at 5:30. Hitchhiked to Bolton and caught bus to Coeburn. Got a cab to bring me to Dan's and I stayed with him. I saw Gene Culbertson's daddy. Cub is in N. Y.

Wednesday, July 19 "Van (*Van Buren Crabtree, brother-in-law*) brought me home this morning. I am lying around, trying to rest up a bit."

This is the last entry in the Diary until September 23. But a lot had happened since Dad entered the Navy and more was about to happen at home in late 1944 and early 1945 that was not recorded in the Diary.

Chapter Nine

Keeping Up The Home Front

The entries made in the Diary from July 4 to July 19 make it clear that Dad was granted an extended leave by Lt. Commander L. F. Loutrel, Jr., Commanding Officer, USS HOPPING, DE 155. This leave, no doubt, was influenced by the other officers on board, Mrs. Hallsted L. Hopping who was active in assisting service men with special needs and especially those who were serving on the Hopping as well as the American Red Cross. What is not revealed in the Diary were the events happening at home.

As mentioned earlier, Dad was 31 years old with six children at home ranging from ages 2 to 14. In fact, according to recent interviews with some of his shipmates, he was known as "the old man" and was actually older than almost all his shipmates and most, if not all, of the officers including the Captain.

His absence created an unusual hardship for both he and our mother. He, because he was away and could not help with the farm work which was essential to the economical well being of the family and mother because she had to manage getting the work done on the farm with very little money and, at the same time, take care of 6 children, 2 girls and 4 boys.

Since it was a time of war and all the young, able bodied men were away, the only ones to perform the farm work were mainly mother and my two older brothers, Charles and Bill, with help from my grandmother. Charles was 13 when Dad entered the navy; therefore, he was the one to whom most of the heavy work fell, such as plowing, mowing hay and harvesting the crops with two large Belgian horses. He was always very responsible and reliable in every task he undertook; therefore, most of the work was completed. Bill was 11 years old when Dad entered and I was 9. Bill was always strong for his age but not always willing to do hard work although he usually carried his load. He maintains, even to today, that he was just working smart instead of hard. I was mainly responsible for carrying drinking water to the fields and doing several light chores such as feeding the chickens and hogs and carrying in wood and coal to fire the cook stove and fireplaces.

Mother worked in the fields along with Grandma. Many times she would take the 3 smaller children to the fields and let them play under and around a shade tree until she had to go to the house to prepare meals. During these most difficult days she remained steadfastly positive and continued to encourage us even though there must have been many times when she felt the loneliness, responsibility and heavy burden of possibly raising 6 children without her husband. On many occasions throughout her life and as we children grew to appreciate what she lived through, we would ask her, "How did you do it?". To which she would always reply that you simply do what you have to do and have faith and trust in the Lord that He will take care of you. Then she would add with a resolute look: "Hard work with a purpose will solve most situations."

Several previous references have been made in the Diary to a telegram. All of these were related to an issue between several supporters of Dad's and the local draft board. There was a strong belief by Dad and his supporters that the local draft board issued draft notices to a select few men who were politically active during the 1943 election. These men were in their 30's and had several children at home while younger men with fewer children were not drafted. This situation led to my grandfather, Daniel Crabtree, seeking assistance from the U. S. Congressman of our district to appeal to the Navy Department for a hardship discharge in order for Dad to take care of the farming chores to provide for his family especially since the war in the Atlantic was nearing an end. All efforts to obtain a hardship discharge were rejected by the local draft board as such requests had to meet their approval. Again, it appears that political differences decided the outcome of the request.

Since the hardship discharge had been declined, probably the ship's captain, Lt. Cmdr. Loutrell, made the decision to extend Dad an additional 30 days emergency leave to allow him time to help with the farm chores during the prime farming season of June through August. The USS HOPPING, in the meantime, left New York on July 18 with Cort Div 6 to escort 41 ships to Lisahally, N. I. and returned to Berth #3, N. Y. Yard Annex, Bayonne, New Jersey on August 15, 1944.

Each time the ship returned to New York there were dances organized by the ship's service committee. They looked forward with great anticipation to the dances which provided them respite from the long hours at sea and provided an opportunity for the officers and enlisted men to come together off duty and off ship. The dances were well attended by both officers and enlisted men and everyone with whom I spoke remembered them fondly. The dance following their return on August 15, was held at the Hotel Roosevelt on August 22. It is interesting to note from the following invitation, that this dance was specifically for "an enlisted man" and a lady guest. I found no record that Dad ever attended one of these dances.

> SHIPS' DANCE
>
> This invitation is for a lady guest with an enlisted man who has been invited to the
>
> HOTEL ROOSEVELT—HENDRIK HUDSON ROOM
> Madison Avenue and 45th Street
> New York City
>
> Tuesday, August 22, 1944 at 8:30 P. M.
>
> SHIPS' SERVICE COMMITTEE

In addition, a 1944 menu is included from the "Paddle's Resturant and Bar" where some of the men may have taken their dates for dinner. The prices may look inexpensive compared to today's but certainly not compared to their pay of $30-$60 per month. Also note at the bottom of the page for "SPECIALS FOR TODAY." There were strict ceiling prices imposed by the federal government's O.P.A. (Office of Price Administration.) The menu had a very large selection which should have satisfied most appetites.

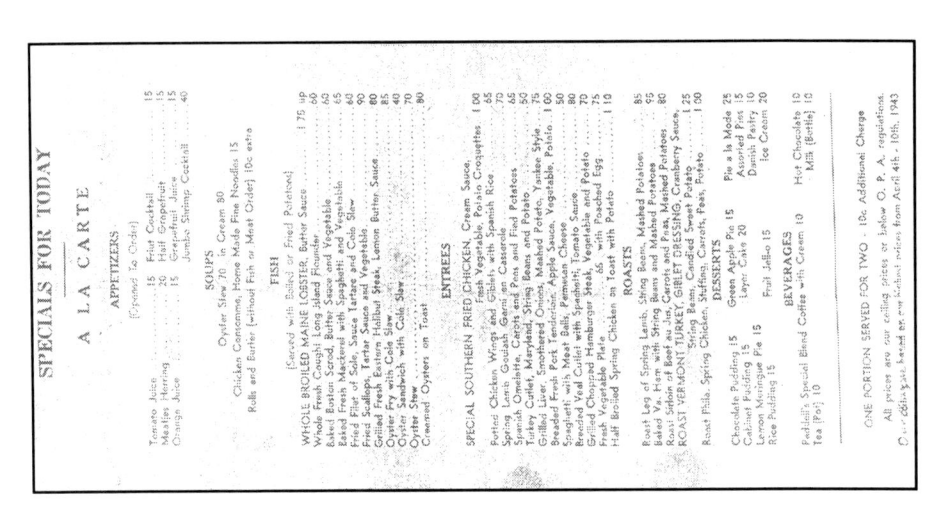

Paddell's Menu, 1944

Paddell's Menu Cover, 1944

At home in far away southwest Virginia it would have been difficult for us to relate to dancing and dining in such "luxury" because life was simple and the work was hard. The chores on the farm continued with or without Dad's presence because crops don't wait for man's schedule. However, when he was home more work was accomplished. The work day usually began with a hardy breakfast around 5:30 a.m. immediately followed by feeding the horses and milking the cows, along with other necessary chores. Work usually began in the fields around 7:00 a.m. before the day became too hot. "Dinner" was at 12:00 noon and it was another large meal usually with 2 meats, several vegetables from our own garden, corn bread and lots of milk. Work continued at 1:00 until 5:00 or 6:00 p.m. depending on what had to be completed for the day. After that the animals had to be fed, milked and cared for along with the other chores to get ready for the next day. Then we gathered for supper and completed the day with family games that we invented for entertainment. Some of the games were geography quizzes, states' capitols quizzes, spelling bees and math challenges. Before bed we all gathered around the radio to get the war news update for the day. Unlike today's newscast, the journalists were always uplifting the United States with good news. They told the accomplishments of the fighting forces abroad as well as giving us the latest progress regarding the war efforts at home and we received encouragement from the President or some other respected official. The news journalists and political leaders were more in tuned with the welfare of the people and the nation than the self-ingratiating and political motives of today's reporters and politicians.

During this time that Dad was home on emergency leave, a particular incident happened that seemed to increase Dad and Mom's resolve to make it through these difficult times and to cause changes at the local level when the war was over.

The incident began when Uncle Van Buren Crabtree loaned Dad, without charge, one of his large coal trucks to make a trip to Spartanburg, S. C. to purchase a truck load of peaches to bring back to the area and sell them by going house to house. This was to provide extra money for the family to purchase basic food and farm supplies. However, word spread to the local draft board members that this was taking place over about a 5 day period and it was considered a violation because the leave was supposed to be for the purpose of doing work on the farm. The draft board reported this to the Navy Department and requested disciplinary action be taken against Dad. This further separated the two political sides and caused "hard feelings" between individuals for years to come.

Dad returned to his ship on August 17, 1944 and resumed his duties on board. Therefore, no disciplinary actions were taken against him by the ship's captain.

Hopping Officers, Sept. 1943

back row L to R
Wenzel-communications
Miller-First Lieut.
Daly-asst.gunnery
Gibbons-supply

front row L to R
Hargrave-asst. eng.
Loutrell-Capt.
Brinn-Exec.
Brown-gunnery

HOPPING OFFICERS
SEPT 1943

Lt. Cmdr. L. F. Loutrel, Jr. was relieved of command of the USS HOPPING on August 16 by Lt. Willard J. McNulty, the Executive Officer. The USS HOPPING, with Dad aboard, participated in exercise maneuvers from August 23 to 26 in preparations for another convoy duty across the Atlantic. They departed New York on August 27 for Lisahally, Northern Ireland with a convoy of 47 ships. On September 7, the Hopping moved to Utah Beach and deposited the convoy. From there the Hopping went to Spithead, Portsmouth, England with another convoy of ships and the next day returned to Cherbourg, France where they anchored inside the outer seawall. Captain McNulty attended a meeting on Utah Beach where he received routing instructions. On September 13, the Hopping, along with Cort Div 6 ships began forming a convoy of 54 ships to return to New York, arriving on September 23.

For the next ten weeks, the USS HOPPING, DE 155 would be under conversion to an APD at Frontier Base, Tompkinsville, Staten Island, New York.

Saturday, September 23 "We pulled in today from England and France."

Since this voyage ends the service of the USS HOPPING, DE 155 in the Atlantic it is appropriate at this point to include copies of two poems someone on the Hopping wrote which depicts the life and attitude of its crew. The poems reveal typical G. I. humor, positive attitude, loyalty to their shipmates and patriotism.

THE HOPPING

We were cruising down the English coast
  One dark and dreary day,
We had 0630 revielle,
  In the same old Hopping Way.

Our purpose is to form a screen
  For convoy ships protection.
But the only thing that's on our mind
  Is "Annual Military Inspection."

Our mighty bow plowed through the surf,
  Old Glory at the mast.
This is an ambitious fighting crew,
  So we'll "turn to" at last.

We're here to escort those mighty ships,
  They're sure a fine collection.
But we have no time to think of them,
  It's "Annual Military Inspection."

At last the spell is broken,
  As the French coast comes into view.
The Soundmen have a contact,
  And we're ready for "G.Q."

The Hopping crew was very tense
  They're really on the ball.
We dropped the charges - killed 'em all,
  Light bulbs, sea weed, fish, and all.

But never fear, you folks back home,
   Through this war may later come depression,
Our Victory will come real soom.
   "Cause we'll pass the "Military Inspection."

"Cause we're trained to be content,
   And keep our ship real pretty.
So when we hit a foreign port,
   We look like <u>Gentlemen</u> from the "City."

We realize our minds are bent,
   And we don't mind how time is spent.
We don't even mind being underpaid,
   Always VICTORY FIRST - then the parade.

Author Unknown
USS Hopping DE 155 Year 1944

D-E DUTY

Have you ever stood on the flying bridge,
   With the spray going over our head?
When you try to sleep in your sack at night,
   You bounce to the very overhead?

When "chow" is called in the morning,
   Believe me it;s no thrill
To sit down to a cup of "Joe",
   When the darn thing won't hold still.

The way she pitches and tosses,
   Makes your head go 'round and 'round.
And you hang over the fan tail,
   While your belly turns upside down.

I suppose you think I'm talking,
   Of some storm far out to sea,
To you battleship sailors it would be calm,
   But it's not when you're on a D-E.

Now don't think I'm complaining,
   Or that I want to squawk,
But believe me, mate, if I had my way,
   I'd darn sight rather walk.

So as you sail on smoothly,
   Please give a thought to me.
I'll still be getting tossed around,
   Aboard this <u>damn</u> D-E.

Author Unknown
USS Hopping DE 155 Year 1944

Lt. Laverne Bordwell, Chief Engineering Officer, the "mustang", had a special talent other than being an excellent engineer officer as evidenced by the following painting of the USS HOPPING, DE 155.

For the next month, there are brief entries in the diary but not every day.

Tuesday, September 26 "I left for home today at 5 P.M. on 60 hour liberty."

Wednesday, September 27 "Arrived home at 1 o'clock today."

Thursday, September 28 "Left back for N. Y. this morning at 6 o'clock. Me & Violet."

Friday, September 29 "Arrived at Staten Island this morning at 4 o'clock. Got a room at the Evelyn Lodge, 71 Central Ave., Staten Island, N. Y."

It is amazing to me what a person will do when he really wants something! It is approximately 730 miles from New York to Clintwood, Virginia. That's 1460 miles round trip in 2 ½ days on slow moving trains with at least three transfers plus hitch hiking the last few miles home!

Saturday, September 30 "We went to Coney Island today and had a nice time." (*This entry was made by Mother.*)

Tuesday, October 3 "I went to the Naval Hospital today for an examination. Got back at 3:30."

It is possible the examination was related to the hardship discharge request but this cannot be confirmed. He was in excellent health at this time.

Wednesday, October 4 "It is pretty cool here. Me and Violet are going out to find her a coat, going to Richmond Ave."

Wednesday, October 11 "We went to Madison Square Garden to see Roy Rogers in person. This was the prettiest place I have ever seen." *(Another entry by Mother.)*

Thursday, October 12 "We went down to the ship this evening and were making plans to come home." *(Entry by Mother.)*

Friday, October 13 "We left Staten Island this evening at 4:30 o'clock. Got to N. Y. City about 5:30 and left for home at 6 o'clock." *(Entry by Mother.)*

Saturday, October 14 "We arrived at home today at 4 o'clock." *(Entry by Mother.)*

Sunday, October 15 "Truman, Maggie, Fred and Nervia went over to grandma's today." *(Entry by Mother. "Nervia" was my paternal grandmother's nickname or shortened version of Minervia.)*

Monday, October 16 "We dug potatoes today." *(Entry by Mother.)*

Saturday, October 21 "Maggie, Nervia, Truman and me went to Pine Creek today to the church conference and to church at Flemingtown tonight. Truman led in prayer tonite. Seems good to hear him pray again." *(Entry by Mother.)*

Once again, this is the last entry in the diary until March 2, 1945; however, there were more things happening at home that must be shared.

The specific dates of the following cannot be confirmed because there are no known records; therefore, what is presented is from my memory as well as my brothers, aunts and a couple of friends whom I interviewed.

Sometime between October 21, 1944 and November 19, 1944, Dad reported back to the Hopping for duty in preparation for departure to the Pacific. Shortly thereafter Mother became gravely ill and was admitted to the local Phipps Hospital in Clintwood. This was the only hospital to care for the people in Dickenson County at the time. Dr. Rufus Phipps, a graduate of the University of Virginia Medical School, was the owner and only doctor. His daughter, Jean Luie Phipps, was the only nurse. Dr. Phipps had a most respectable reputation for the care he provided his patients and is remembered as having performed many wonderful services in the community. Dr. Phipps determined that Mother's illness was gall stones and needed immediate attention. An operation of this nature in 1944/1945 was extremely serious and especially in the small, less equipped and understaffed hospital. Everyone I interviewed remembered Dr. Phipps and Grandpa Daniel sitting by Mother's bedside all night because Dr. Phipps was concerned she would "not make it through the night". He performed the surgery to the best of his ability but did not remove the gall bladder as is done in today's surgery. This was confirmed in 1998 at the age of 87when she had another gall stone attack and the bladder was removed. We children remember the 12-15 gall stones were kept in a glass container in the china cabinet for several years following and we remember shaking them to hear them rattle which intrigued as well as amused us. Also, she remained in the hospital for at least 30 days before coming home for an extended recuperation period.

Obviously, during this period with Dad in the navy and Mother in the hospital, we six children had to be cared for. Charles, being the oldest, stayed on the farm with Grandma to take care of the animals. Bill spent some time with Mother's sister and her husband, Magdalene and Donald Dotson. I went to live with Mother's brother and his wife, Mack & Zetta Crabtree. As best we can remember, the three youngest, Anna, Buford (Boots) and Fern, went to live with Grandpa Daniel and Aunts Josephine and Merlin. Our stays lasted about 3 to 4 months, probably from December through March when Mother had recuperated sufficiently to care for us again. It was a difficult time for all of us and for those family members who cared for us. It was also a time that is embedded in my memory for the love shown to our family by Mother's family. But we survived and were made stronger for having had the experience.

Another incident occurred during the spring of 1945 which we older children remember well and it was confirmed with Mother before her death. After 58 years we cannot remember the exact date but it was about the same time as the Battle of Okinawa, March 27 - April 21. We knew Dad was in the Pacific where fierce naval battles were taking place with Japanese forces although we did not know his location.

It was a nightly occurrence for my Grandma and cousin, Catherine Branham, to visit us in the evenings to check on Mother's recuperation progress and to have a family prayer for Dad. As Grandma and Catherine were leaving our house one evening we gathered on the porch to say good night when we all heard the most "Angelic" choral singing coming from the family cemetery about 200 yards from our house. It was indescribably beautiful! We listened for about 10 minutes before it faded away. None of us could identify the song. Mother and Grandma held prayer for Dad and Mother reassured us that God had sent His Angels to let us know that Dad was alive and safe. As we now know, he was wounded at Okinawa on April 9. Within a few days after we heard the singing, Mother received a telegram saying he had been wounded! I believe God had His Angels watching over Dad, Mother and us six children at a time when we needed His protection.

Springtime meant the plowing, planting and preparations had to be done for the coming growing season. Charles, who was almost 15 years old now, had to do most of the heavy work especially with the horses. He remembers having to plow not only our gardens and fields but also several neighbors' gardens and fields. All the while we all attended school regularly. In fact, Charles said he would get up early enough to plow for a couple of hours before he walked about 1 ½ miles to school arriving in time for the first class at 9:00 a.m.

My intention has been to present, in the preceding pages, just a "peek" at what life was like for our family at home while Dad was contributing his part to preserving our freedom from the tyranny of world despots. Looking back now we children still view our situation then as a responsibility we had to each other, our family, community and nation. There was a sense of true patriotism toward our country and what it was fighting for. Our parents did not expect our government to do any more than to direct our nation's efforts toward victory in order to preserve our way of life and we realized that our way of life, our freedom was worth our efforts.

As a family and individually we grew stronger by facing the challenges and realizing a worthwhile victory for all people. In retrospect, it was a wonderful time in which to grow up. It taught us invaluable lessons of independence and a true sense of self worth as well as an appreciation of a strong work ethic and the importance of a family sticking together.

Chapter 10

Converting The Hopping To An APD And Off To The Pacific

As noted in the previous chapter, October 21 was the last entry in the Diary until March 27, 1945. Therefore, I have had to rely on several sources, especially the ship's WAR DIARY and Muster List; a brief "History of the USS HOPPING, APD-51" from the Officer of Public Information, Navy Department; "History of Transport Division 105", an uncopyright account, written by J. M. Kennaday, Captain, USN, Commander Transport Division 105; Lieutenant William H. Wenzel, Communications Officer who was aboard the Hopping from July 20, 1943 until October 30, 1945 and notes and interviews with other Hopping shipmates. All of these sources have been invaluable, especially to cover events when the Diary was "dark".

The USS HOPPING, DE 155 spent some ten weeks in dry dock on Staten Island, NY being converted to APD 51. This conversion was necessary because it would be serving with the Pacific fleet for the remainder of the war where the need was for high speed personnel transports of underwater demolition teams (UDT) for the purpose of laying demolitions on the beaches for the invasion forces to land on the islands that were heavily fortified by the Japanese.

The following excerpt, giving a description of a converted APD, is taken from, **Tempest, Fire & Foe**, by Lewis M. Andrews, Jr.:
"APD's were destroyer escorts and World War I type (four piper) destroyers altered to have light troop transport capabilities. They were created by two opposite but complementary situations. The first was a need for light transports with relatively shallow drafts and a capacity to move light army or marine units rapidly to myriads of Pacific islands. The second was a growing excess of destroyer escorts in the Atlantic,

permitting several to be converted.

Another deck was added along with troop berthing and messing accommodations for about 10 officers and 150 men. A very large davit was installed on either side, each of which could launch and recover two 36 foot assault landing craft (LCVP). It could carry underwater demolition teams (UDT) or move troops, supplies, light trucks and jeeps to and from the staging areas. The 3"/50 caliber main battery was replaced with a more efficient destroyer type 5"/38 caliber gun forward in a movable mount. Torpedoes, hedgehogs and K guns were removed. The sound gear and depth charges in stern racks remained to leave the APD with a reduced antisubmarine capability. Additional 40mm and 20mm guns were installed to increase the ship's close-in antiaircraft armament.

The destroyer escorts played a major role in breaking the back of the German and Japanese submarine fleets and, together with APDs, contributed heavily to the defense against the *kamikaze* corps. From North Africa to Anzio to Normandy, across the broad reaches of the Atlantic and Pacific Oceans, from Leyte to Iwo Jima to Okinawa to Tokyo Bay, their crews cheered, laughed, fought, bled and died."

It took the navy yard from September 23 through November 18 to complete the conversion during which time the officers and men were either on leave, housed in the Prince George Hotel in downtown Manhattan, attending schools or assigned other details.

The Hopping's WAR DIARY begins again with the following entries:
"*19 November 1944*
0600 Underway with aid of three tugs to Mariners Harbor, Staten Island, NY for dry docking.
0815 Dry docked in dock 7."

20 November 1944
1230 Dock flooded and inclination test performed.
1600 Underway with aid of three tugs to US Naval Frontier Base, Tompkinsville, NY.
1800 Tied up at base.

ONI 226/1 • CONFIDENTIAL
Division of Naval Intelligence

HIGH SPEED TRANSPORTS (DE CONVERSION) APD

US

Operational use	To transport and land raiding or reconnoitering troops close to the landing beach.
Description	50 TE and 50 TEV type DE's have been converted to APD's of this group APD 37-86 are ex-TE's, APD 78-136 are ex-TEV's.
Capacity	4 LCVP (4 davits), 150 troops, 4 carts TPL, four 75 mm pack howitzers, 4,500 cu. ft. cargo ammunition, 3,500 cu. ft. general stores, 1,000 cu ft. gasoline.
Dimensions	Length, 306'. Beam, 37'.
Displacement	2,043 tons (full load). Draft 12' 7" (full load). 14' 0" (with sound dome down).
Armament	One 5"/38 cal., three 40 mm twins, six 20 mm.
Endurance	5,000 miles @ 15 kts, 2,000 miles @ 23 kts.
Speed	23 kts. (max.).
Propulsion	Turbo-electric drive.
Crew	203 officers and men.

21-25 November 1044
No change.

26 November 1944
0730   Underway from Frontier Base.
0830   Moored pier 1, Leonardo Pier, Earl, NY taking on full allowance of ammunition.
1445   Underway, various courses and speeds.
1545   Moored degaussing (demagnetizing) station, Bayonne, NJ for de perming.

27 November 1944
0745   Underway from degaussing station standing out of New York Har bor on various courses and speeds conforming to the channel.
1100   Compensated compasses and swing ship off of Ambrose light.
1400   Conducted structural firing in same area expending 4 rounds 5" 38, 48 rounds 40mm and 120 rounds 20mm.
1530   Proceeding back to US Naval Frontier Base, Tompkinsville, NY using various courses and speeds conforming to the channel.
1745   Moored stbd side to south side pier 9, berth 5 and 7.

28-29 November 1944
No change.

30 November 1944
2400   Reported for duty as APD."

The USS HOPPING, DE 155 was now officially USS HOPPING, APD 51!

The newly converted ship with crew sailed from Frontier Base at 0935 on December 1, 1944 bound for Norfolk, Virginia arriving at 0930 on December 2. At 1400 the ship's captain, Lt. Cmdr. McNulty, called on the Chief of Staff to received orders for shakedown exercises in the Chesapeake Bay.

The shakedown and training exercises began at 0847 on December 3 and lasted through December 13 when they moored port side to

USS HOPPING, APD 51

USS CROSLEY, APD 87, north side of pier 7, NOB, Norfolk, VA. until December 20.

On December 20 at 1210 the USS HOPPING, APD 51, was underway from Norfolk with the USS ANNE ARUNDEL, USS LYON, USS DOROTHEA L. DIX and USS BUNCH, DE 694/APD 79, to Cristobal, Canal Zone arriving on December 25 and anchored in Limon Bay, C.Z.

They were underway again on December 26 and began their voyage through the Panama Canal completing it on December 31 when they entered the Pacific Ocean enroute to San Diego arriving there on January 3, 1945 along with the USS BUNCH, APD 79.

After a five day lay over in San Diego, the USS HOPPING, USS BUNCH and the USS RINGNESS, APD 100, operating as a Task Unit, departed on January 9 for Pearl Harbor, Territory of Hawaii. The three ship TU arrived at Pearl Harbor on January 15 and reported for duty with the Pacific Fleet.

On January 17 the Hopping, operating independently and under secret orders, conducted a "full power run" exercise and made a trip from Pearl Harbor to Mau Laeu Bay, Maui in 5 hours and 1 minute where it reported for duty and training in underwater demolition work. For the next 27 days the Hopping participated in training exercises with UDT 17, UDT 19 and UDT 4. These exercises were conducted at Anaehoomalu Bay, Hawaii; Mau Laeu Bay, Maui; Becks Cove, Kahoolane Island; Mallaeu Bay, Maui; Smugglers Cove, Kahoolaweth; and Keulaikuhileii Island.

UDT Invasion Maneuvers

UDT Invasion Maneuvers

Truman at the Gun

Hopping Crew at Sea
(Joe Best and Truman, far right)

Hopping Crew with Hawaiian Natives

Hawaiian Native Hut

    This scene portrays that their life was not "all work and no play". Their time in the Hawaiian Islands must have provided them a welcomed and deserved respite.

UDT at Liberty

Lt. William Wenzel, the communication officer, had this to say about their training experiences in Hawaii:

"There we had exercises with other ships, had gunnery practice off the various islands with liberty on the 'big island' and in Maui. One such exercise had us drop depth charges which explosion resulted in a sizable fish kill. A crew was sent to pick up the fish which were then cleaned by the mess cooks and we had a fish fry and beer picnic on shore the following day. This included a crew's softball game with rather unique rules, requiring a runner to finish off a beer before advancing to the next base. Abner Doubleday must have turned over in his grave! The game was called due to not being able to hit the ball or even see it in some cases."

Hopping Gun Crew

Also Lt. Wenzel had the responsibility of teaching the crew to recognize Japanese aircraft and ships by sight. I was able to confirm that the following pictures were the ones he used in his teaching sessions:

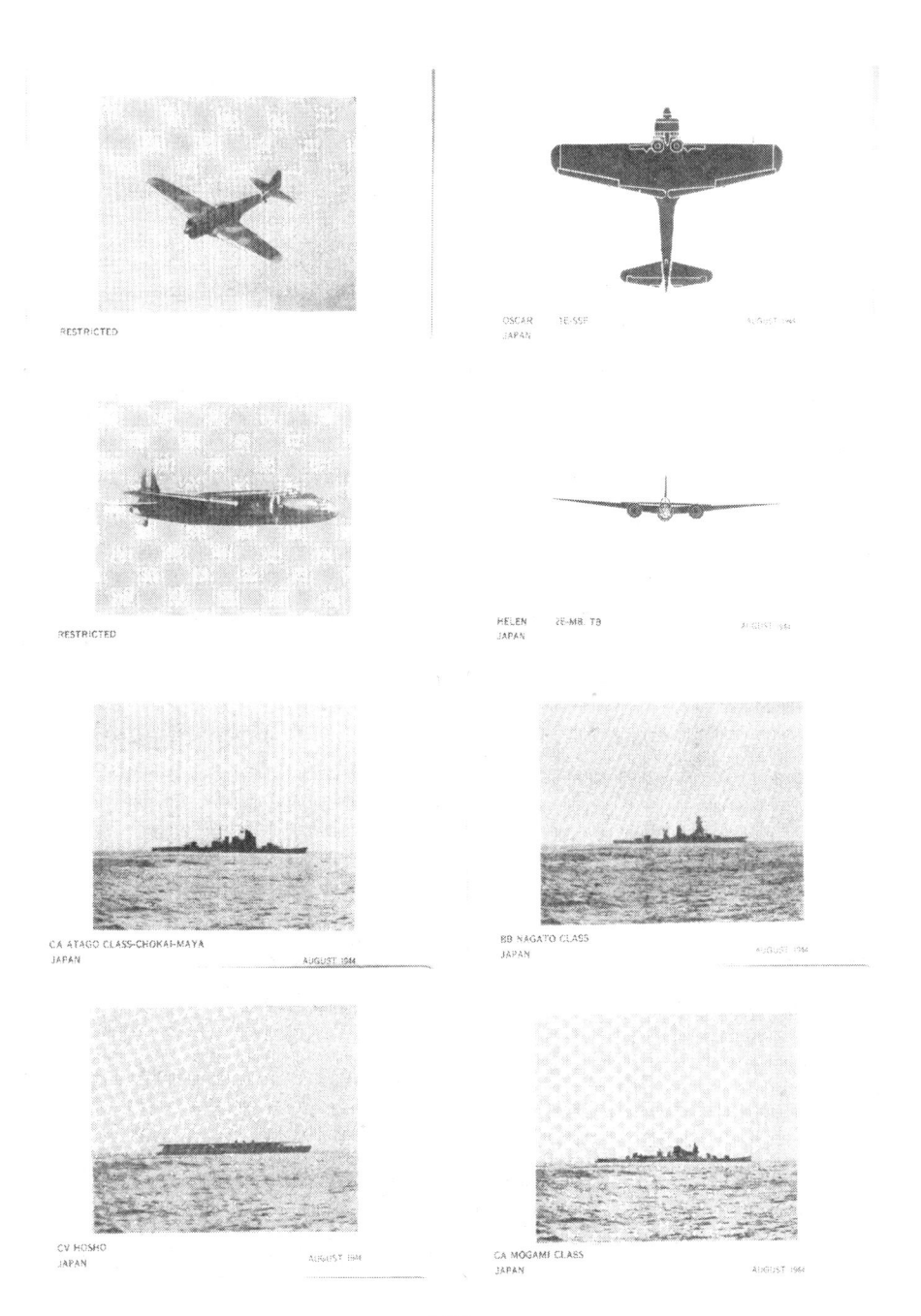

RESTRICTED

OSCAR   1E-S5F
JAPAN

RESTRICTED

HELEN   2E-MB. TB
JAPAN

CA ATAGO CLASS-CHOKAI-MAYA
JAPAN   AUGUST 1944

BB NAGATO CLASS
JAPAN

CV HOSHO
JAPAN   AUGUST 1944

CA MOGAMI CLASS
JAPAN   AUGUST 1944

Before moving on, it is noteworthy that the Hopping, Bunch and Ringness traveled alone to Hawaii and, for the most part, conducted their training exercises independently. There was good reason for this that dates back to the beginning of their transport division. In early January, 1945 Transport Division 105 staff was formed in Norfolk and the following ships were assigned to its command: USS BARR, APD 39; USS SIMS, APD 50; USS HOPPING, APD 51; USS REEVES, APD 52; USS PAVLIC, APD 70; USS TOLLBERG, APD 103; USS DIACHENKO, APD 123; USS HORACE A. BASS, APD 124; USS GOSSELIN, APD 126. The staff embarked in late January on the Diachenko for San Diego intending to rendevous with the other ships in Hawaii. However, the division commander, Captain Thomas C. Thomas, USN, was hospitalized in San Diego. It was reported that a corpsman treated his eyes with a harmful solution that caused irreparable damage and, therefore, he could not continue in command and remained in San Diego. The staff, however, continued on the Diachenko to Pearl Harbor arriving the first of March. By this time the USS BARR had completed its training and had been assigned to the fleet operation at Iwo Jima. The USS HOPPING and USS REEVES had been assigned to proceed to the Phillippines for further preparation for the invasion of Okinawa. The USS SIMS was still in Hawaii. It was determined that the USS DIACHENKO was to be separated from the rest of the division and sent to the Seventh Fleet in Southwest Pacific except the division staff was to be shifted to the USS SIMS. Both the Diachenko and Sims left Pearl Harbor in early March in escort duty to Okinawa. On March 17, Captain J. M. Kennaday, USN, relieved Captain Thomas as Commander of Transport Division 105 and boarded the USS GOSSLIN. The Gosslin and Bass departed Hawaii for Ulithi and Okinawa together. The Pavlic left Hawaii April 13 on escort duty to Majuro, Ulithi and Okinawa . The Tollberg was on her way to the Central Pacific and didn't rejoin the division until they were entering Tokyo Bay.

From this time until the war ended, the ships of Transport Division 105 were mostly separated and operated under several different commands while performing different duties as needed. However, Captain Kennaday remained as the commander of the division until the end of the war. He served on different ships of his division and six of the division ships, under his command, were among the first US ships to enter Tokyo Bay immediately following the Japanese surrender.

The final exercise in Hawaii for the Hopping began on February 12 when she loaded approximately 41 tons of tetrytol and was assigned to Task Unit 13.11.13 which was composed of the following eight ships: USS BUNCH, USS HOPPING, USS KLINE, USS GRIFFIN, USS CROSLEY, USS LOY, USS HERNDON and USS REEVES. On February 13 the Hopping embarked UDT 7 composed of 84 men and 12 officers with Lt. Cmdr. R. Burke in command of UDT 7 and proceeded to Maalaeu Bay, Maui for AA firing practice and on February 14 left Maui for Eniwetok Atoll, Marshall Islands and Leyte with TU 13.11.13. They crossed the international date line on February 18, arriving at Eniwetok Atoll on February 22 where the ship fueled to capacity and took on provisions.

Once again Lt. William Wenzel, communications officer on the Hopping, shared another interesting experience. "Only one day was spent in Eniwetok where we took on fuel and replenished our supply of food from a supply tender. Movies were also exchanged at the 'tender' with those we had already seen. Movies were the principal entertainment now. They were shown on the fan tail whenever we were in port, either at anchor or tied to a berth. The other entertainment was swimming off the ship when we were at anchor in a quiet bay. Somehow the riflemen who stood watch for sharks when swimming went on didn't have a comforting effect on me! When underway, we frequently listened to Tokyo Rose on short wave radio. Rose was a US citizen who broadcasted from Japan to US troops and ships intending to destroy their morale, speculating about the fidelity of their wives and sweethearts they had left behind in the US and warning them of the gruesome things awaiting them at their next attempted invasion of the Pacific Islands. Listening to Rose was a way to learn more about the progress of the war, as we had little other information. Most servicemen took these broadcasts as amusing. The main reason for listening, however, was for the music. Rose had all the US hit tunes by all the leading bands and vocalists. Tokyo Rose's counterpart in propaganda in the Atlantic theater was Axis Sally, another US citizen turned traitor. Both Rose and Sally were convicted of treason after the war and served prison time.

The supply ships frequently had fresh fruits and vegetables and ice cream mix. We ate well! Fresh milk was the item most missed. When expressing their dreams, sailors would say, 'The first thing I'm going to do when I get back to the States is have a great big chocolate milkshake.'"

On February 23, the Hopping received verbal orders from Commander, TU 13.11.13 to report for temporary duty to TU 96.3.17 to become one of six APD's to escort 44 ships from Eniwetok Atoll to Kissol Roads by way of Ulithi. The convoy arrived at San Pedro, Tarrraguna, Leyte Gulf, Phillippines Islands on March 4, 1945. TU 13.11.13 had completed its mission and was dissolved. The Hopping was then assigned to Phib Group 7 and on March 7 and 8 the commander of UDT's Phibs Pac held several meetings with all commanders in the Task Group regarding forthcoming training period and operations.

Dad's Diary begins again with the following entry in a small pocket sized, leather covered notebook:

March 2, '45 "6:15, 4:30 A. M. Home. We passed by the Yap Islands, 20 miles off. Feb. 28 by Yahoma I. March 2 was payday + shots. $30 on books. Arrived Leyte March 3, 1945, Sun. Air raid Sun. Nite at 4 o'clock in morn."

They were underway on March 9 in accordance with Com UDT's Phibs Pac Top Secret rehearsal operation with other APD's, DD's, LCI-GC, LCI-Ms7. For the next seven days they trained, held tactical drills and made dummy landings off Taytay Point in preparation for the invasion of Okinawa.

On March 18 the WAR DIARY had an entry that caught my attention. It read, *"1135 Anchored in berth 324, San Pedro Bay, Leyte, P. I. By accident all current key lists were burned. Made reports to Com Trans Div 104, Com Phibs Pac, and Op Nav. Replaced key lists."*

Since I had served as a cryptographer in the US Army I knew these were the top secret codes for the upcoming invasion operation, they were of the utmost importance for the protection of the ships, crews, UDT's and success of the invasion. Also, I was aware that in military operations only the facts are presented......not the details of what happened. Therefore, I began to seek an answer as to what happened to these top secret documents and again Lt. Wenzel came through.

"As a result of her conversion from a DE to an APD, the Hopping now had space for one hundred-fifty troops (UDT teams) in addition to the usual ship's crew of about two hundred officers and men. As a APD we now carried four small landing crafts (LCVPs) along with rubber rafts used by the frogmen to go beyond the landing craft and to hold their extra supplies and equipment as they worked in the water. We held training exercises with them in the Phillippines for about two weeks, learning how to launch the landing craft from our ship and setting up a communications system for the ship to the landing craft and to the men on the rubber rafts. A lot of coordination was required and a lot of practice was needed to achieve this.

While in the Phillippines, other preparations were made for the upcoming invasion. The communications officers from all the ships in our group, for example, were given instructions on the communications to be used during the operation and a complete set of new codes was issued to each ship.

I took my set back to the Hopping and was busy inserting them into our code book. This was a three-ring binder, of the usual type, except the cover which was made of lead. The idea being if we were ever in danger of being captured, the code book was to be thrown overboard where it would sink rather than fall into the hands of the enemy. This book was always kept in the small code room. There was little space or equipment in this room. The Electric Coding Machine (ECM) was there. This looked much like an electric typewriter. However, it had a set of about ten bakelite and copper disks which were inserted into the machine in a sequence prescribed by the code in effect at the time. This garbled a message so if one were to type 'the quick brown fox' it came out in five letter groups something like, 'zpqte revol acywt debxm'. Then someone receiving this message and having their ECM disks in the proper order would type in the garbled letters and out would come 'the quick brown fox'. We had a schedule of when to change the sequence and which disks were to be inserted. Also in the code room were codes for other types of messages, signals, etc. In addition there was a waste basket and a 'burn bag' that was made of heavy canvas. It had numerous grommet holes and a draw cord at the top. It too was weighted with a piece of lead similar to the note book and for the same purpose. All decoded messages and any other 'top secret' documents no longer needed, were put in this 'burn bag' for destruction by burning. This bag hung from a hook welded to the bulk head in the code room directly over the waste can. A straight-backed chair completed the furnishings.

While putting the new codes in order, I balanced the code book on top of the waste can. There was no shelf or desk available. I had a knock on the door and a yeoman informed me the executive officer, Lieutenant Ed Hargrave, wanted to see me in his office. I locked the door and on my way out of the radio shack, encountered Ensign Lehman, who was now assigned as my assistant communications officer. He told me he had been granted some liberty and was going ashore for a few hours. I asked him to take the 'burn bag' ashore and to burn the contents and also to check with the ship's office to see if they had anything to burn as well. They had a 'burn bag' like the one I had in the code room for all classified waste paper accumulated.

When I finished my visit with the Executive Officer, I returned to the code room to complete the job. NO CODE BOOK! There was a limited choice of places to look, and I had a pretty good idea of what had happened. I rushed back to the Exec and told him what I thought had happened. He allowed me to go ashore and I practically ran to the disposal sight. No Ensign Lehman! Back I went to the Exec. I was really worried. Here were the codes to be used for the invasion –missing!! This could compromise the entire operation, should they fall into the wrong hands. I suggested that I report this at once to the Division Communications Officer. Hargrave said I was getting too upset and suggested I wait for Lehman to return. I waited in panic. It seemed hours went by. I thought of all the horrible consequences. Finally Ensign Lehman returned to the ship, and I asked him if he'd seen the code book. 'Yes', he said, 'I wondered why you wanted it burned and couldn't figure how to dispose of the lead cover as it wouldn't burn, but we (he was with the Chief Yeoman) felt it wouldn't matter since there was no printing on it anyway.' Well, at least we now knew it had not fallen into improper hands. I went to the Division Communications Officer, told my sad story and requested a new set of codes. None were available. 'How will I decode any messages?' I asked. 'We'll relay them to you if there is anything you need to know or that involves the Hopping. Otherwise, I'll get a set to you if and when I can.' This helped some, and it was good to know I wasn't going directly to Portsmouth Navy Prison for neglect of duty, or whatever the charge might be, but it was the most stressful event I'd ever been involved in up to that time in my life."

According to the Hopping's WAR DIARY the key lists were replaced and the Hopping, along with five other APD's and ten DE's and DD's, formed Task Group 52.13 and departed Dulag, Leyte, Phillippines Islands on March 21 escorting 20 transports to Kerama Retto, a small group of islands about 15 miles west of Okinawa. During the voyage of five days they destroyed several floating mines with 20MM fire. Upon arrival on March 26 they left their transport ships at anchor a safe distance and began their screening duties during which they were called to GQ (General Quarters or battle stations) four times that day and observed three enemy planes shot down.

Tension was beginning to mount because they were already seeing action even though the invasion was not to officially begin until April 1 and they were only three hundred fifty miles from Japan facing the island of Okinawa which was heavily fortified with over 100,000 fanatical Japanese soldiers plus the Japanese air force with its fighters, bombers and kamikazes along with a sizeable naval force awaiting orders on the mainland to come to the aid of Okinawa.

For the next several days the training, skills, courage and determination of the crew of the USS HOPPING, APD 51would be tested to the ultimate during the Battle of Okinawa or 'Operation Iceberg' as it was known and which British observers described as "the most audacious and complex enterprise yet undertaken by the American amphibious forces".

Chapter 11

Dad, The Hopping and the Battle of Okinawa

Dad begins to record again on March 26 and continues through April 13.

March 26, 1945 "Early this morning we began to see burning fires on the island and shell fire. GQ at 3:30. Jap planes came over. Four (4) of them and all were downed all around us. They sent 100 out and lost 100. We had two ships hit."

March 27, 1945 "At 4 p.m. we went to Okinawa Jima and watched the bombers, battle wagons, cruisers bombard the beach. Could see towns burning. We were close to beach. There was plenty of protection for us (planes)."

March 28, 1945 "Remember! 3/26-27-28. Saw plenty action. A Jap suicide was down by our side."

The Hopping's recording of this states that the plane was a "Val" or Japanese dive bomber. Three ships commenced firing on it and it crashed 10 feet astern of the USS CROSLEY and a short distance from the Hopping!

March 29 "I am plenty nervous but something to remember. All nite big bombers were diving on us dropping fish and bombs. At day break a suicide boat was blown up. Two of them and plenty enemy aircraft. A horrible nite this was. Today the UDT is going for reconnaissance at 8:30. It is 7:30 - 29th. Remember always. GQ all nite & day."

113

The Hopping's WAR DIARY confirms and elaborates on Dad's brief comments:

"29 March 1945
0040   Flash White.
0102   Flash Red.
0110   "Val" dropped two small bombs 100 yds to port.
0114   Twin engine plane, probably a "Betty", dropped bomb 400 yds ahead. Both planes were fired on when it was apparent that they were attacking. No results observed. Although the night had bright moonlight it was impossible to see planes over 3000 yds. Ship held fire to about 1800 yds. As soon as firing commenced all hands were blinded by the tracers from the 40MM. Night magazines on 20's have no tracers.
0142   "Betty" attacked from ahead, dropped bomb 100 feet on port bow. Vigorous fire from Hopping.
0213   "Betty" crashed about four miles away in flames.
0345   Opened fire on "Betty" driving it away. It is believed that this plane hadn't seen us until shipopened fire.
0457   Flash Blue. Ship goes to general quarters for all Flash Reds. Expended during the evening 4 rounds 5"38, 230 rounds of 40MM, 938 rounds of 20MM.
0520   Dawn, G. Q.
0553   Sighted "Val" just within gun range. Held fire. "Val" went on his way.
0615   Plane down several miles to north.
0620   Flash Blue. Ordered to join TG 52.13, left patrol station.
0637   Observed USS BUNCH and USS CROSLEY destroy two suicide boats about a mile ahead. Boats are low, about 20 ft, plywood, speed about 8 knots, one man crew and explosives. They are defenseless in the daytime, their only protection is darkness.
0800   Proceeding with TG 52.13 and under the immediate command of CTG 52.11, Captain Hanlon Com UDTs Pac to the western beaches of Okinawa Jima.
0909   Lowered boats at R hour - 21, 6000 yds off Yellow Beaches. UDT 7 embarked for reconnaissance of Yellow Beaches. Operation supported by BB's, CA's, CL's, DD's, DM's, LCI (G)'s, LCI (R)'s and LCI (M)'s. Patrolled off beach at 6000 to 8000 yds. Support ships inside 5000 yds.

1037   Flash Red.
1109   Flash White.
1142   All boats back UDT 7 completed mission satisfactorily. USS HERNDON and USS CROSLEY had teams in at same time.
1200   In afternoon USS BUNCH, USS LOY and USS KLINE's teams scouted beaches with same support. Herndon, Crosley and Hopping screened seaward.
1950   Took inner A/S screen station in Fire Support Group formation for night retirement."

To assist in understanding the fire power referred in the preceding log, the following brief descriptions are presented: A "Betty" was a Japanese Mitsubishi Zero or fighter plane. A "Val" was a Japanese dive bomber. These were attack/fighter planes - not suicide planes. A "fish" was a torpedo. As you can see, from 1:00 a.m. to 6:00 a.m. the Hopping encountered at least six attacks by these planes and all were at night when they came low over the horizon in order to get as close to the ship as possible before being seen. On the US side, the abbreviations mentioned at 0909 hours are: BB-Battleship; CA-Heavy Cruiser; CL-Light Cruiser; DD-Destroyer; LCI (G)-Landing craft, Infantry (Gunboat); LCI (R)-Landing craft, Infantry (Rocket); LCI (M)-Landing craft, Infantry, (Motor). One needs to keep in mind that this action was only in preparation for the invasion or L-Day scheduled for April 1 and this was composed of about one-fifth of the operation. There were about 172,000 US combatants and 115,000 US service troops at Okinawa under the command of Admirals Raymond Spruance, Marc A. Mitscher, Raymond Kelly Turner and Lieutenant General Simon Bolivar Buckner, US Army. All were performing their assigned duties extremely well and in a very coordinated fashion. There were over 1400 warships operating off shore Okinawa at this time ready to land over 160,000 army and marine assault troops and I read several accounts by observers who stated that there were warships "as far as the eye could see". It is interesting to note that there was more armament, materiel and personnel assembled for this invasion than for the invasion of Europe on D-Day. This armada must have been an incredible sight!

March 30, 1945 "Today was a sorrowful day because of all the bombing. It took place all day. Not much enemy resistance. 7:30 P.M. here Friday - about day break at home."

March 31, 1945 "A few air raids today. We are in anchorage tonite. Tomorrow is Love day - Easter."

The Hopping notes during this time that they were on GQ almost 24 hours a day and while proceeding to anchorage off Kerama Retto on March 31, they observed a dead Japanese who was a one man crew of a suicide boat. He was clothed in a one piece suit, helmet and life jacket. It appeared to them that he intended to swim away from the suicide boat. Also, attached to his body was a long red sash about 12 feet.

April 1, 1945 "The invasion of Okinawa this morning and history was made. For me, such an experience. I have never seen A.A. fire like this. It was awful. Four vals downed. Two bombs and fish were dropped at us, only a narrow miss. I counted 164 American fighter planes. GQ all nite again."

The Hopping's WAR DIARY entry for this day:

1 April 1945
"Underway from Kerama Retto as part of TG 52.13, CTG 52.13, Capt. R. D. Williams ComTrans Div 104. Under orders of CTG 52.11 is Op. Plan 3.45. Numerous Flash Reds during the day. Four Thousand yards off the Western Beaches of Okinawa observed three Jap planes shot down, firing on one of them. Transferred officers and men from UDT 7 to various control craft for the purpose of guiding in the initial waves of the Okinawa Jima assault.
0800   L 26-27N 127-27E
0830   Invasion on. Returned to Kerema Retto to fuel and then back to Okinawa. Recovered UDT 7 personnel then took up screening station."

April 2, 1945 "You should be hearing from this about now. Its 8:30 A.M. here on Monday. Sunday, 1st there. We sure are seeing plenty of action out here. Love, back home."

SPECIAL CINCPAC COMMUNIQUE AS OF 1200 GCT
APRIL FIRST, 1945

The United States Tenth Army whose principal ground elements include the 24th Army Corps and the Marine 3rd Amphibious Corps invaded the west coast of the island of Okinawa in the Ryukyus in great force on the morning of 1 April (East Longitude Time.) This landing is the largest amphibious operation of the war in the Pacific to date.

Admiral R. A. Spruance, USN, Commander 5th Fleet is in overall tactical command of the operation. The amphibious phase of the operation is under command of Vice Admiral Richmond Kelly Turner, USN, Commander Amphibious Forces Pacific Fleet. The Tenth Army is under command of Lieutenant General Simon Bolivar Buckner, Jr., USA.

The landings were made by ships and landing craft of the U.S. 5th Fleet supported by the guns and aircraft of that Fleet.

The attack on Okinawa has also been covered and supported by attacks of a strong British carrier task force, under Vice Admiral Sir Bernard Rawlings, against enemy positions in the Sakishima Group.

Troops of the 24th Army Corps are commanded by Major General John R. Hodges, USA, and the Marines of the Third Amphibious Corps are commanded by Major General Roy S. Geiner, USMC.

The attack on Okinawa was preceded by the capture of the island of the Kerama Group west of the southeastern corner of Okinawa which commenced on 26 March. The amphibious phases of this preliminary operation were commanded by Rear Admiral Kiland, USN. The troops consisted of the 77th Army Division under command of Major General Andrew D. Bruce, US. The capture of these outposts was completed prior to the main landings on Okinawa and heavy artillery is now emplaced there and in support of the Okinawa attack.

The amphibious support force is under the command of Rear Admiral W. H. P. Blandy, USN, who was also present at the capture of the Kerama Group of Islands and in general charge of these operations. The battleships which form the principal gunfire support elements are commanded by Rear Admiral M. L. Deyo, USN.

Fast carrier task forces of the U.S. Pacific Fleet which are participating in the attack are under command of Vice Admiral Mark A. Mitcher, USN. The escort carriers which are supporting the attack are under command of Rear Admiral C. T. Durgun, USN.

More than 1,400 ships are involved in the operation. The landings were preceded by and are being covered by heavy gunfire from battleships, cruisers, and light units of the U.S. Pacific Fleet. U.S. carrier aircraft are providing close support for the ground troops. Strategic support is being given by the shore based air forces of the S.W. Pacific Area, Pacific Ocean Areas, and by the 20th Airforce.

The operation is proceeding according to plan. The troop who went ashore at 0830, Tokyo time, advanced inland rapidly and by 1100 had captured the Yontan and Kadena airports with light losses.

The capture of Iwo Island gave us an air base only 660 miles from Tokyo and greatly intensified our air attack on Japan. The capture of Okinawa will give us bases only 325 miles from Japan which will greatly intensify the attacks of our fleet and air forces against Japanese communications and against Japan itself. As our sea and air blockade cuts off the enemy from the world and as our bombing increases in strength and proficiency our final decisive victory is assured.

This was Dad's last entry until April 9. I will abbreviate the Hopping's entries until then.

"2 April 1945
During the hours of darkness many Flash Reds and much AA fire around the horizon. At daylight closed beach and transferred UDT personnel for days work. The sea is full of ships going in every directions. About 1900 hrs USS DICKERSON, APD 19 was hit by suicide plane in bridge area. USS BUNCH and USS CROSLEY assisted in control of fire and stood by until tug took the Dickerson in tow."

April 3, 4 and 5 they were off the beach during the day and screening at night. Then they moved to the southwest end of Okinawa.

"6 April 1945
Screened USS Estes in morning, entered Nakagusuku Wan (later Buckner Bay) in afternoon to look over Red Beach on Tsugen Jima. Spent most of the afternoon and evening at general quarters. Much enemy air activity. Observed six planes shot down. The only near one being a suicide attempt on the USS WICHITA in which the plane's left wing was shot off."

"7 April 1945
Ordered to search for downed Mariner by CTG 51.19. Search til daylight in area southwest of Okinawa, results negative. In morning debarked UDT 7 who made reccon. of Red Beach on southwest end of Tsugen Jima. Team completed mission successfully and returned to ship. Operation supported by five DD's, the USS LAMS and USS BUDGER. No opposition."

"8 April 1945
Patrolling off entrance of Nakagusuku Wan in morning. USS ESTES and USS WICHITA plus destroyers, mine sweeps and two mine layers in harbor. Approximately 0815 one of the mine sweeps hit a mine and damaged bow so severely that ship was beached. In afternoon another YMS (auxiliary mine sweeper) exploded a mine under its stern and was towed off."

Auxiliary Mine Sweeper

Auxiliary Mine Sweeper

Lt. Wenzel shares his observations aboard the Hopping during these dangerous days: "It was several days after the invasion of April 1st before Japan responded in force. The first massive attacks against the US Fleet came April 6 and 7th. Literally hundreds and hundreds of planes were sent to attack our ships. Over one hundred US ships were damaged or sunk. Most of these ships were those on picket duty. Then, to supplement the Japanese fighters and bombers, the suicide planes were used.

UDT on Okinawa

Results of Bombardment

This would be Japan's last attempt to hold off invasion of the home islands. This situation was one of desperation for the Japanese. Young Japanese men were recruited for suicide missions. This was called the kamikaze plan, the 'Divine Wind', which was to bring honor in death to those who died, along with their families. Their mission was simple. Fly the short distance from Japan to Okinawa and crash into any US ship they could find. Volunteers were given the most basic flight training in obsolete planes with 550 pound bombs aboard and only enough fuel to get there (not enough to get back should they change their minds). They took off to attack US ships in Okinawa waters for their last act of bravery. Over two thousand of these suicide missions were made before the Island was conquered.

Japanese Pill Box on Okinawa

Japanese Cave on Okinawa

Kamikaze attacks were unforgettable. It was difficult enough to defend against a fighter plane attack but to fight a kamikaze was even more difficult since their objective was to die. The usual plan of attack was to fly low to the water and typically from either a rising or setting sun. This made the planes difficult to see, due to the bright sun and hard to pick up on radar because of the low altitude. Only one in five got through the anti-aircraft fires, but the four hundred seventy-five that did get through caused tremendous damage. The Hopping was under kamikaze attack many times. Doing all that could be done in taking evasive action; zig-zag turns, changing speed and firing all guns that could be brought to bear and praying a lot, ("for those in peril on the sea") was all that could be done. The rest was pure luck. We were never hit by one of these pilots on a suicide mission, but they surely scared us a lot! We'd frequently see an attack on a nearby ship who would respond with anti-aircraft fire. Sometimes an explosion, either the plane or on the ship. Mostly a splash next to the ship, a near miss or a crash caused by a hit by gunfire. Then it would be over and quiet for a time, until another plane would attack. Maybe your ship this time.

The Hopping was able to paint several Japanese flags on her bridge for 'kills' made before the operation was over."

The WAR DIARY continues:
"9 April 1945
0100   *USS ESTES left the formation, Com Cru Div 4 in USS WICHITA the OTC. Screened until 0930 when ship entered Nakagusuku Wan for reconnaissance of Purple and Brown Beaches on the northwest side of the bay. The cruisers and destroyers in the bay bombarding shore installations. UDT 7 completed reconnaissance.*
1415   *The Hopping stood by awaiting orders, in the meantime the USS PENSACOLA bombarded Tsugen Jima with her main and secondary batteries. Ordered by Com Cru Div 4 to take up A/S screen off Nakagusuku Wan, proceeded out past Tsugen Jima when an unknown shore battery opened up and hit our port side six times; 3 times with 75CM and 3 times with 4.7 inch shells.*

Damage as follows: 5 holes in side of ship, three support girders amid ship's frame 96 shot away, washroom smashed up, air cooler to after generator holed and leaking, one starter coil to after main generator holed and leaking, one starter coil to after ship's service generator cut, main bearings after generator wiped, a Mark 14 sight was holed, door knocked off a booby hatch, numerous electrical and piping casualties. When the shell went through the fireroom, cutting a steam line, the boiler was secured, which cut the steam to the oil pump. The automatic relay cutting in the electrical pump worked but the breakers jumped out thus leaving the main generator with no lubrication while it ran down. Both after fire room and after engine room were full of steam due to broken steam lines, thus the ship only had power on one screw. The chief engineer, Lt (jg) L. A. Bordwell, USN, at great personal risk, entered the engine room three times to get the steam secured. After the engine room was free of steam, the ship was put into two motor control. The ready 40MM guns took the shore battery, which was about 2000 yds off, under fire immediately and the 5" joined in when the crew got to general quarters. When the ship opened fire the shore battery stopped. As the USS WICHITA and USS PENSACOLA steamed out they too covered the area thoroughly. Expended 29 rounds 5" 38, 148 rounds 40MM. It was found that the power lead to the davit motors had been cut so that the boats couldn't be used until a casualty power line was lead out. It is recommended that these motors have power leads from both the forward and after power panels.

Personnel casualties were: UDT 7, KIA 1, WIA 8, ships company KIA 1, WIA 10. Four of the wounded were transferred to the USS MOBILE in the evening.

2000   *USS Hopping joined astern of the USS Wichita, USS Pensacola, USS Mobile screened by two destroyers."*

Dad's entry for this day was brief. It was exactly one year ago this day that he boarded the Hopping.

April 9, 1945 "At 4:45 this eve. I was hit with shrapnel from shore battery. We lost two men. On sick list."

Lt. Wenzel recalls his experience of this day. "Sometime we were taken from the picket line to escort a ship from one anchorage to another or for us to refuel at sea. Then we'd be reassigned as a picket ship in a new location. On April 9, we were doing picket duty off of 'Buckner Bay'. This bay on the south coast of Okinawa, had been named in honor of General Simon Bolivar Buckner who lead the Army and Marines in the invasion. He had been killed in action at this location. It was bright, sunny day. No enemy planes had been in the area for hours. Those of us not on watch were resting in our bunks. 'Bong, bong, bong–Now hear this! All hands, General Quarters! Man your Battle Stations!' I grabbed my GQ gear and raced to the bridge to my battle station. Captain McNulty was already there. He explained, we had just taken several hits from a shore battery and told me to maneuver the ship so that we could fire our five-inch gun in the direction the shell came from. Meanwhile, the 'talkers' reported from the stern that several men had been hit and we had several fatalities. All the hits were above the waterline and were not disabling the ship. We fired about six or eight rounds from our five-inch gun and reported our situation to our Division Commander, who asked for air support and got it. A nearby cruiser fired a number of salvos from it heavy guns at the shore battery. Several torpedo planes dropped their charges at the suspected sight and several fighter planes came by and sprayed the area with machine gun fire. They made several passes.

We were secured from GQ and I went below, heading for my bunk by way of the wardroom. There I encountered the ship's doctor, the chief pharmacist and several other pharmacists operating on a man lying on the wardroom table with the bright overhead light shining down on him. I retraced my steps to approach my quarters from another direction. When I walked into my room, I found one of the fatalities lying in my bunk with a sheet drawn over him. Back I went to the signal bridge and had Signalman Pratt rig a hammock for me. There I stayed and what sleep I had the next twenty-four hours was swinging in a hammock.

Lieutenant (jg) Miller, the ship's doctor, reported to Captain McNulty, we had two men killed. One from UDT 7 and one from the ship's crew. Several men had superficial wounds and stayed aboard, while three were transferred to other ships where better medical facilities were available.

One of the injured was a Beta from the University of Minnesota, Ensign Charles Cashman, the 'Boat Officer'. Chuck had been trained in amphib operation at Fort Pierce, Florida and had been assigned to the Hopping in November, 1944. Being one of the more junior officers, he had quarters in the stern section of the ship. He was in his bunk reading when a shell pierced the hull, took off one of his fingers and kept going through the hull on the other side. His first comment was, 'I hope this doesn't ruin my golf game.'

The following is from a letter written by Chuck Cashman describing the action and the series of events he experienced afterward.

"I was one of the guys that got hit by Japanese shore batteries on Tsugen Jima, April 9, 1945. I was hit by shrapnel in both hands and in the chest. Within fifteen to thirty minutes, I was transferred by small boat to the USS Mobile, a light cruiser, for surgery. That was the last I saw of the Hopping. I was in the USS Mobile sick bay for close to three weeks during which time she was engaged in shore bombardment. While I was aboard in addition to the daily kamikaze attacks, the #2 six-inch triple gun mount blew up, killing or injuring some thirty of her crew. Shortly after that, I was transferred to the USS Pinckney anchored in Kerama Retto. The Pinckney was a camouflaged ship used as a troop transport, but then as a base hospital in Kerama Retto. The second night I was aboard the Pinckney, it was hit by a suicide plane, three guys in my quarters were killed along with fifty others of the crew and patients aboard. The ship was severely disabled and I, along with the rest of the patients and crew, had to go over the side.

I was picked up by a boat from an LST that was anchored nearby. The LST was an ammunition ship and when I told the captain of my experiences during the preceding thirty days, he thought it would be bad luck to keep me aboard. I was transferred to the USS McKinley the next morning, stayed there two days and was finally transferred to the USS Hope, a Red Cross hospital ship. We spent two days at the main landing area in Okinawa picking up casualties from the shore and finally got underway for Saipan.

I spent two weeks in the hospital on Saipan and was then flown to the area hospital at Pearl for a month and then transferred by jeep carrier to the Navy Hospital in San Diego, California. I was there when the war ended in August, 1945, and that is where I was discharged from the Navy in November because of my wounds.

I wasn't on the Hopping for long, but she was a good ship and had the best of crews. I am lucky to have served with them.
With my best regards,
Charles E. Cashman"

Chuck returned to Minnesota and graduated from law school at the University of Minnesota. Eventually, he became a district judge and spent thirty years with the court. He added to his letter, 'It is and has been a good life, and it has been interesting.'"

USS HOPE, Hospital Ship

April 10, 1945 (From Dad's Diary) "At 1:30 P.M. this afternoon, we performed the burial at sea. Jurgelionis & Bock. Went to hospital ship 170 A.P.A. this evening." (The ship was the USS GOSPER, APA 170, an attack transport.)

"10 April 1945 (From ship's WAR DIARY)

    Followed formation into Nakangusuka Wan in morning and watched landings of 27th Division on Tsugen Jima. Shore battery opened up again but was silenced by cruiser and DD fire. Transferred three casualties to the USS Estes along with report of beach reconnaissance. In afternoon proceeded to Kerama Retto.

1300 Conducted services for the burial of the dead and buried Julius Francis Jurgelionis MM 1/c and Leonard Joseph Bock, Jr., S 1/c at sea.

1710 Anchored in Kerama Retto. Transferred the remaining casualties to the APA 170."

Jurgelionis was from Worcester, MA. His wife lived at 55 Ellsworth St. and his father at 154 Ingleside Avenue.

Lt. Wenzel gave the following account of the burial at sea. "The following day, we were sent back to Kerama Retto, but on the way were given permission to conduct, 'Burial at Sea'. The boatswains prepared for this by sewing heavy canvas body bags, which were weighted with five inch shells to take them to the bottom. The bodies were placed individually into these bags, which were then sewn shut. These were placed upon wide flat boards which were carried top side forward on the forecastle. The Captain had the entire ship's crew, plus the UDT assembled there. Lieutenant (jg) John Gibbons had been appointed to perform the ceremony, perhaps because he was the only officer aboard with a Book of Common Prayer. Captain McNulty said a few appropriate words. Mr. Gibbons read the words from the prescribed prayer from the Prayer Book devoted to 'Burial of the Dead at Sea", 'Unto Almighty God we commend the soul of our brother (and gave the sailor's name) departed and we commit his body to the deep.' The men supporting the wide board on which the body was placed, raised one end, the body slid from beneath the flag which had been placed over it and into the sea it plunged. Riflemen fired a round from their guns and all hands on board came to a salute. This procedure was performed two times, once for each of the deceased. Captain McNulty dismissed the assembled and we returned to our regular duties. It was a somber affair, leaving all of us speechless for some time, but thinking, 'There, but for the Grace of God, go I'. I'm sure all who witnessed, remember.

'Hear us as we pray to Thee
For those in peril on the sea.'"

Lieutenant Lavern Andrew Bordwell, USN, received the Bronze Star Medal for his outstanding service when the ship was first hit. And the following enlisted men received the Bronze Star Medal for their outstanding service during the crisis: Robert Stanley Phillips, CBM(T), USNR; William Charles Garrow, BM 2/C, USNR; Henry Klekman, Cox., USNR; Robert (Shorty)Morrow Miller, S 1/C, USNR; George Grove, CEM(T), USNR; Samuel Nicastro, CEM(AA)(T), USNR; Robert George Mangeau, MM 3/C, USNR; Harold H. Randall, RdM 3/C, USNR; James Francis Donohue, S 2/C, USNR; Joseph Frank Pazzynski, F 1/C, USNR; and Carl Fred Hamann, WT2/C, USNR. Captain Willard Jerald McNulty received the Silver Star Medal for his outstanding performance throughout the whole Okinawa campaign.

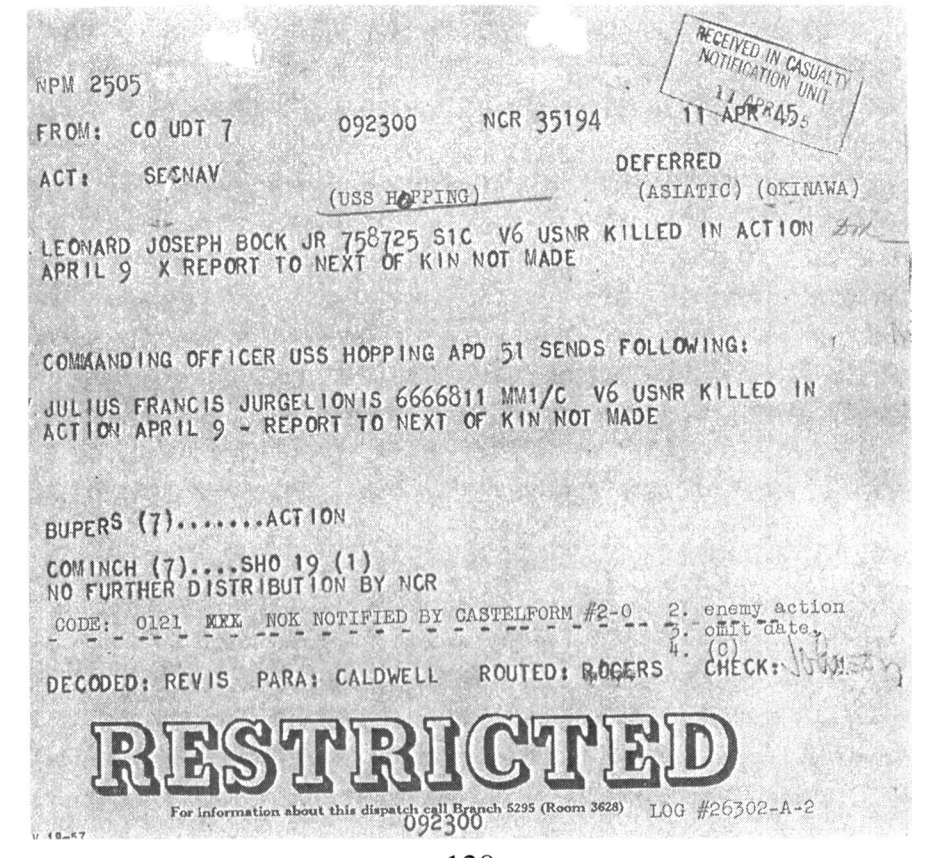

```
NPM 2505
FROM:  CO UDT 7         092300      NCR 35194        11 APR 45
ACT:   SECNAV                                    DEFERRED
                       (USS HOPPING)            (ASIATIC) (OKINAWA)

LEONARD JOSEPH BOCK JR 758725 S1C V6 USNR KILLED IN ACTION
APRIL 9 X REPORT TO NEXT OF KIN NOT MADE


COMMANDING OFFICER USS HOPPING APD 51 SENDS FOLLOWING:

JULIUS FRANCIS JURGELIONIS 6666811 MM1/C V6 USNR KILLED IN
ACTION APRIL 9 - REPORT TO NEXT OF KIN NOT MADE


BUPERS (7)........ACTION

COMINCH (7)....SHO 19 (1)
NO FURTHER DISTRIBUTION BY NCR
  CODE: 0121  XXX  NOK NOTIFIED BY CASTELFORM #2-0   2. enemy action
                                                    3. omit date.
                                                    4. (C)
  DECODED: REVIS  PARA: CALDWELL   ROUTED: ROGERS    CHECK:
```

RESTRICTED

For information about this dispatch call Branch 5295 (Room 3628)   LOG #26302-A-2

Lt. (jg) John Gibbons Conducting Burial Ceremony

Bob Tero Upper Left by Rail

On April 11 both Dad and the Hopping record that Dad was transferred from the USS Gosper back for duty on the Hopping and he makes the following entries:

<u>4/12/45</u> "86 planes attacked. All were downed, did much damage."

<u>4/13/45</u> "I heard of F. D. R.'s death this morning at 7:30 A.M. Flags are half mast for 30 days."

The Hopping received some repairs at Kerama Retto April 11-13 and on April 14 joined Task Unit 51.15.21 in escort duty bound from Kerama Retto to Ulithi, P. I. arriving there on April 23. From April 24 through May 9 the Hopping was moored along side the USS PRAIRE at Ulithi for repairs to battle damage. Also, while moored along side the Prairie, UDT 7 unloaded officers, men, equipment and explosives. They had served their duty and were no longer needed on board the Hopping.

UDT 7 at Troop Landing on Okinawa

The Hopping's Muster List shows that Dad was transferred on April 24 to the USS HAMUL, AD 20, for treatment of wounds; however, his Diary has the following entry: "R. S. Navy 926. I arrived here 24th. Will go on watch tomorrow morning with bakers. On from 1-6 A.M." and the Hopping's Muster List shows that on June 16, 1945 he was transferred at Okinawa from R. S. Navy No. 926 back to the Hopping for duty. Therefore, he must have spent from April 24 to June 16 on

UDT 7 on Okinawa

the R. S. Navy No. 926. I did not search the Hamul's or R. S. Navy No. 926's records for an explanation of the missing transfer(s).

The only other entry he made during this period was apparently from ship No. 926, "May 26, '45, Mailed my watch today at 2 P.M." I can only surmise that he was a very safe distance from the fighting and so relieved that he simply did not make any entries or he was suffering from the wounds and did not want to write about them. He received wounds in the left hand and back.

Meanwhile the Hopping reported ready for sea duty on May 11 and joined Task Unit 94.18.20 as an escort with 13 other ships bound from Ulithi to Okinawa arriving there on May 17. On arriving at Okinawa the Hopping took up screening and patrolling duties in addition to relieving other ships of their duties.

Throughout the action at Okinawa the screening/patrolling/picketing duty performed by the Hopping was on the outer edges or a few miles away from the supply ships, war ships and other service ships that were conducting the bombardment and invasion of the mainland. This duty was extremely dangerous and it was where the US had the most damage done to its fleet because it was the first defense against the incoming Japanese fighters, bombers, kamikazes, warships and submarines. Also, in carefully reading the WAR DIARY and comparing it to a map of Okinawa and the many islands surrounding it, I discovered that the Hopping was on duty almost everywhere around the main island, i.e., Kerama Retto, Hagushi Beaches (where the main assault occurred), Tsugen Jima, Nakagusuku Wan (Buckner Bay), Zampa Misaki (Point Bolo), Ie Shima, Menna Shima, Ryukyo Retto, Kume Shima, Chimu Wan, and Thuken Jima where the Hopping was hit by the shore battery.

For the sake of brevity, a summary of activity for the Hopping from May 17 through September 4 will cover the main events.

On May 20 two Vals attacked USS HARRY HUBBARD in station B-14. The Hopping opened fire at 7000 yds range. Results unknown due to amount of fire the Hubbard was putting up.

I have in my possession an original copy of the "HOPPING HOKUM" printed on May 21, 1945. It consists of eight legal sized pages and mentions Mrs. Halstead Hopping and Robert Hopping Wood as honorary plank owners. It also states that Robert Hopping Wood, as the youngest member of the Plank Owners Association, was two years old on this date. The birthday menu consisted of cream of turkey soup, soda crackers, celery sticks, cranberry sauce, roast turkey, sage dressing, giblet gravy, mashed potatoes, green peas and carrots, ice cream with caramel sauce and cake, bread, butter, lemonade, cigarettes, candy and cigars. It also contains lots of good humor, cartoons, recollections of dances

Ship's Dance, Hotel Empire, March 8, 1944

at the Rialto Ballroom and the ship's party at Palm Gardens "just a year ago tonight" and news from back home. The copy is in excellent condition.

Ship's Dance, Palm Garden, May 29, 1944

On May 30, investigated a native canoe containing family of ten, three goats and household belongings bound for Menna Shima. Ordered to let them proceed. Again on May 31 at same station, another canoe crossed to Menna Shima. Upon investigating they, too, were allowed to continue.

June 4, awarded eight Purple Heart Medals to men wounded in action on April 9.

June 6 - 8, granted three days availability to clean boiler in Haguski Beach area and received Captain J. M. Kenneday, USN, Commander of Transport Division 105 aboard.

June 14, shot down two drones.

June 17, while anchored at Hagushi Beach a stick of bombs was dropped through the smoke on the anchorage but caused no damage.

June 21, Okinawa was announced secured as of 1305 hours; but the shooting kept up.

June 22, while at anchor at Nakagusuku Wan (Buckner Bay), took a low flying Zeke (Japanese Zero or fighter plane) under fire at about 4 miles. Plane came straight until about 3500 yards and turned away at 3000 yards. It was later shot down by the USS ELLYSON when it attempted a suicide attack. Since the ship was at anchor and the plane came from dead ahead the smoke from the guns became so dense halfway through the run that fire had to be checked.

June 25, from 8:30 p.m. on, there were constant bogy raids and they observed the eclipse of the moon.

July 18, received standby orders to execute Typhoon Plan X and underway from Buckner Bay in escort duty to guide ships to safe distance from the typhoon. They returned to Buckner Bay on July 21.

The last entries made in Dad's Diary were:

<u>July 19th</u> "This morning we left the Buckner anchorage for the typhoon. It wasn't too bad."

<u>July 20, 4:30 P.M.</u> "It's much quieter now. We had a 38 degree roll last nite at 6 o'clock."

Lt. Wenzel gives his recollection of the typhoon. "We were told to join with our Division and head south as a typhoon was predicted. The captain had us at General Quarters. Soon the wind began to howl and the rain came in torrents.

Typhoons hit Japan and the Pacific Island each year between May and November. The winds became violent. Seventy-five miles per hour winds are not uncommon and they have been reported up to one hundred-fifty miles per hour at the eye of the storm. The winds demolish buildings, rip banana groves to shreds and snap off the trunks of palm trees in these typical Pacific typhoons.

I have no idea of the actual velocity we encountered but it lashed up gigantic waves. It became impossible to hold the course set by the Division Commander. He wisely told each ship in his group to strike out on their own to take the best course they could for their own circumstances and that we would regroup after the storm was over. Some groups who attempted to stay in formation lost ships due to capsizing or breaking apart. In fact, even some of the larger ships, not in formation, sustained terrible damage. Aircraft carriers were forced to launch all of their planes as they could not be kept secure on deck. The carrier, Pittsburgh, lost over one hundred feet of her bow during the typhoon along with a number of her crew.

Soon the captain ordered all but a few of us who were on the bridge to go below for fear they would be washed overboard. The waves became mountains. The bow would dive into a wave and the ship would be carried forward, not by the force of the engines, but by the force of the wave. Then the stern would be completely out of the water, the twin propellers would scream as they raced in mid-air with no water resistance to slow them down. We would hit the next wave with such force the mast would shake back and forth like a whip and the siren and the whistle, which were mounted atop the mast, would sound erratically as the cable which controlled them would become taut and then slack.

The worst action came not as we ran into the waves but if one should catch us broadside. The ship would roll on her side and we wondered, 'Would it right itself this time or keep on rolling?' All hatches and port holes were securely battened down. At times the entire hull would be underwater and then it would rise up like a submarine about to surface. Green water would cover the entire deck from stem to stern then run off in a huge gush. We were but a toy in the sea. Anything that wasn't battened down securely was thrown around wildly. Some things were lost over the side.

To move from one place to another was next to impossible. Instead of being on the open bridge, the Captain and I, as OD, were now in the enclosed CIC or chart room next to the helmsman, Quarter Master Barnes, in order to give him commands as it was impossible for him to hear course changes through the voice tube.

Morning finally came and with it some lessening of the wind. There were none of our ships in sight. The rain had stopped but it was still a very heavy sea, not the mountains it had been, but broadside courses were still to be avoided. Gradually conditions improved. The mess cooks were able to feed the crew and the crew was able to eat although the galley was a disaster. Things were slowly returning to normal.

One felt as though he had been in a rough football game for hours on end. Our legs especially hurt from the constant strain and shifting weight from one leg to the other as the ship pitched and rolled. We were bruised where we had been thrown against tables, tubes or what else had been in our path.

We headed back toward Okinawa, sighting a few ships from our group. Short wave radio was used to contact others and our group reformed again. None of our ships had any substantial damage and no men had been lost.

> 'Hear us when we pray to Thee
> For those in peril on the sea'"

On July 26, 1945 Dad was transferred from the USS HOPPING, DE 155/APD 51 for the last time at Buckner Bay, Okinawa to the USS KITTSON, APA 123 for transportation to San Francisco, California for discharge. He had served on the Hopping since April 9, 1944. The war was finally over for him and he was on his way home but the war was not over for the USS HOPPING, APD 51.

Securing and occupying Okinawa greatly helped bring the leaders of Japan to face their inevitable surrender. They had lost over 107,000 men killed, nearly 28,000 entombed in caves and more than 10,700 prisoners.

While the United States had taken a heavy toll, with a total of 12,513 killed or missing in action and 36,600 wounded, this would be the last great battle of the war and as Prime Minister Churchill stated in a cable to President Truman that it would be remembered as "among the most intense and famous of military history."

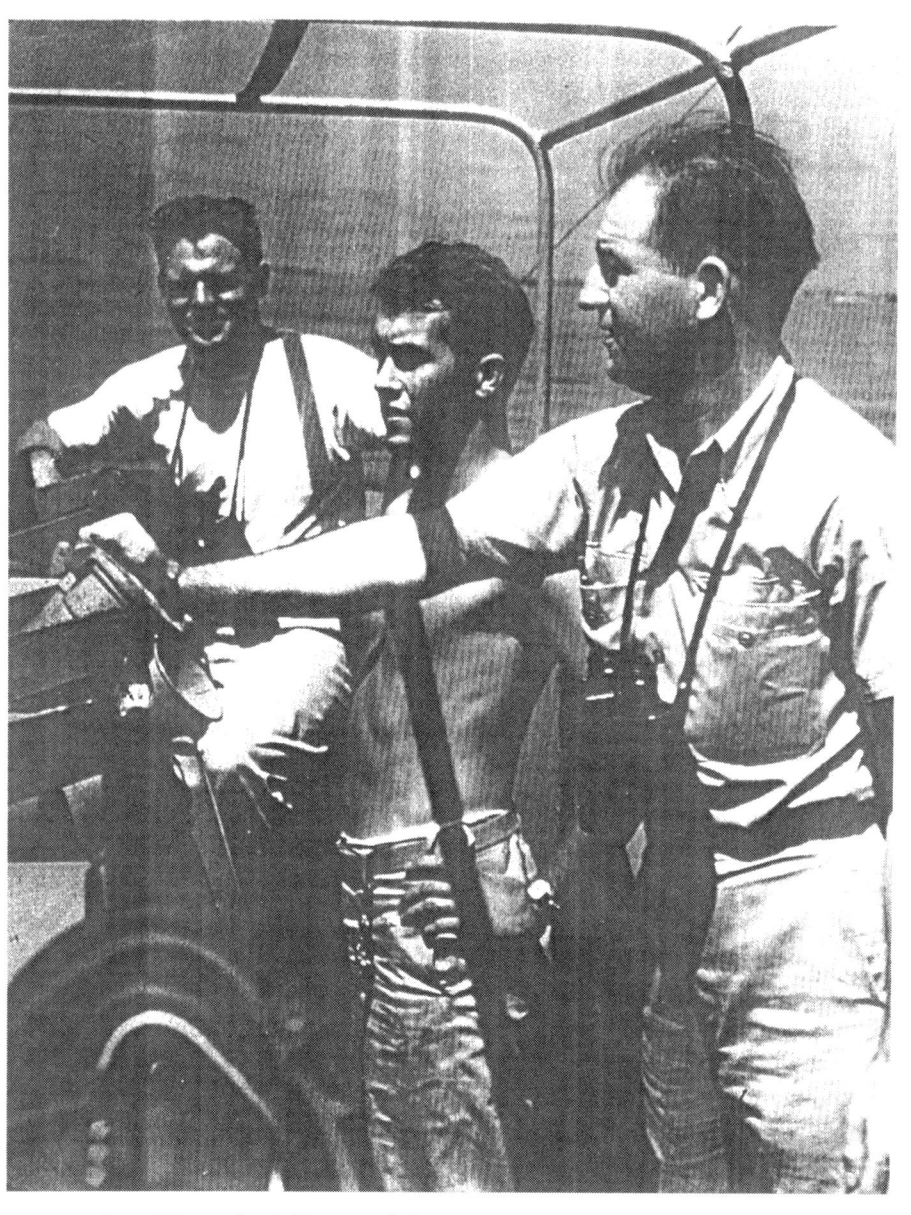

Lt. (jg) Wenzel, Officer of the Deck; Ensign Bennett, Supply Officer; Lt. Bordwell, Engineering Officer aboard the USS HOPPING, APD 51.

Chapter 12

The USS HOPPING, APD 51, From Okinawa To Tokyo Bay And Home

For the remainder of July and August the Hopping continued to conduct screening and patrolling around Okinawa except for an escort trip to Leyte, P. I. and returning to Okinawa. During this time, the US had dropped the atomic bomb on Hiroshima, August 6 and Nagasaki, August 9 and ushered in the "Atomic Age". On August 10 Japan announced agreement to peace terms and the official surrender took place on the USS MISSOURI on September 2, 1945 at 0904 hours.

B 29's on Bombing Raid to Japan

3rd US Fleet Aircraft Carrier

*USS MISSOURI, BB 63, Enroute to Japan
for Surrendering Ceremonies*

US 3rd Fleet in Buckner Bay, August 10, 1945
Celebrating News of Japan's Surrender

    Eight ships, not including the Hopping, of Transport Division 105 under the command of Captain Kennaday, formed an escort for the Third Fleet and sailed on August 18 for Honshu, Japan. The USS REEVES, APD 52, as a part of Trans Div 105, was the first US ship in Tokyo Bay and on August 29 arrived at Omari Prison Camp to liberate the allied prisoners with war correspondents and Commander Harold Stassen on board. One of the prisoners was Marine Ace Major "Pappy" Boyington who had been reported dead; another was the gunner/radioman of Colin Kelly's plane; and they brought out the crew of the first B-29 that was shot down over Japan. Then on September 1 the Reeves was the first ship to enter the inner harbor of Tokyo Bay with war correspondents broadcasting to the United States the situation in Japan. This action was really the first time Trans Div 105 had participated as a group since they were formed back in Norfolk, VA.

Following the liberation of prisoners in Tokyo Bay the Reeves was dispatched to Nagasaki with the Command Team of the US Strategic Bomb Survey crew aboard arriving on October 26 to survey the site of the atomic bomb. The following pictures were made by Hy Sheiner, a crewman on the Reeves, when the ship visited Nagasaki just over two months after the atomic bomb was dropped.

Japanese Colonel Aboard USS REEVES as Escort into Heavily Mined Tokyo Bay

Hy Sheiner from USS REEVES. October 26, 1945 at Nagasaki's Atomic Bomb Site

Nagasaki's Atomic Bomb Ruins

On September 3, 1945 the Hopping received orders to report to Commander, Fifth Fleet, Admiral Raymond Spruance to sail as an escort from Okinawa to Tokyo and on September 5 they loaded supplies in preparation for duty as an evacuation ship for POW's. On September 7 the Hopping was assigned to Task Unit 56.5.2 under the command of Rear Admiral R. J. Riggs, USN, aboard the USS MONTPELIER. TU 56.5.2 sailed on September 9; however, the Hopping was ordered to wait for six medical officers and to obtain batteries for the unit. They were underway at 1700 hours to join TU 56.5.2 bound for Wakayama, Japan and joined the TU at 1000 hours the next day. The TU was made up of the following ships: Montpelier, Lunga Point, LaSildo, Taney, Consolation and Sanctuary. The escorts were: McGinty, French, Putum, Doyle, Cofer, Cockrell and Hopping.

The Task Unit arrived on September 11 at 0600 where they were joined by a mine sweep group. The mine sweep group went ahead and commenced sweeping. Task Unit 56.5.2 formed into one long column and for the remainder of the day proceeded at various speeds on a northerly course up Kii Suido behind the sweeps, anchoring at Berth B 17, Wakanoura Wan, Honshu, Japan.

On September 15, the Hopping received on board 139 ex-POW naval officers and enlisted men who had been captured early in the war in the Phillippines and took them to Guam, arriving there on September 19 at 1331 where they were met by medical officers and buses at the dock and took charge of the RAMPs (Recovered Allied Military Personnel).

In my conversation with Captain McNulty at a ship's reunion in Orlando, Florida in 2001 the subject of these ex-POWs came up. I inquired about their condition and he recalled that they were in piteous condition, emaciated and rather reluctant to talk about their prison life. The very first thing they did when on board was to take a shower and change into clean clothes provided by the Hopping. They wanted to know what was happening back home. Since their safe evacuation was a top priority for the Hopping, they were given the best treatment and services the Hopping had to offer. The mess galley was open 24 hours and they were given the best food available. One shipmate shared that, to him, the "sea ration" he ate during this trip were even good just so these men could have what they wanted and could eat from the ship's galley. He said some could only consume small portions at a time. During this conversation, I casually asked Captain McNulty if all of the ex-prisoners made it back to Guam. His countenance change dramatically as he related that four died on the way. It was very obvious that this hurt him deeply. I then asked if they were buried at sea, to which he responded emphatically, NO! He continued that they cared for their bodies and delivered them to Guam to be returned to the United States for proper burial services. Their mission was to get all of these men back home, even the deceased!

Of all my conversations with Captain McNulty and other shipmates who were on the Hopping during this evacuation, this and the burial at sea were the strongest emotional expressions exhibited by any of them. One can only imagine their deep feeling of loss. And as was said earlier, maybe this is why the veterans are reluctant to share their experiences with those of us who have never had similar experiences.

Two days after delivering the RAMPs to Guam the Hopping was underway bound for Wakuyuma, Japan again in company with the USS FRENCH, DE 367 arriving on September 25. From there they moved to Tokyo Bay and anchored of Yokohama, Japan until October 12 when they were assigned to Task Unit 34.8.9 to escort 8 APAs (Attack transports) and 5 AKA (Attack cargo ships) to San Pedro, Phillippines. They were in the Phillippines, shifting from San Pedro to Manila Bay, Luzon until November 2 when they obtained personnel from the receiving station and left Subic Bay bound to Yokohama, Japan in escort of 15 LSTs (Landing ship, tank) and 1 LSM (Landing ship). On November 3 the convoy encountered a tropical storm resulting in 3 LSTs being damaged to the point they had to return to port for repairs and the convoy lost 36 hours steaming time. They arrived and moored at berth 7, Yokahama Inner Harbor on November 14. They shifted berth to Yokosuka on November 19 and on November 24 underway from Berth 4 Yokosuka, Japan for Pearl Harbor, Territory of Hawaii, steaming independently WITH HOMEWARD BOUND PENNANT FLYING!

Due to heavy seas and poor weather forecasts for the area ahead, they put in at Midway on November 29 for fuel rather than chance running empty. They only stopped long enough for fuel and left Midway 4 hours later for Pearl Harbor. The ship was carrying 150 passengers back to the United States. They arrived in Pearl Harbor on December 4 and departed on December 5 bound for San Diego, California!

The Hopping arrived in San Diego Harbor on December 11, moored south side Broadway Pier, debarked passengers and cleared customs, then shifted to the Repair Base for five days voyage repairs. Got underway on December 17 for the Canal Zone. It is ironic that on December 25, Christmas Day, the Hopping was once again passing through the Panama Canal but this time they were returning from many days of General Quarters, fighting off many attacks from Japanese fighters, bombers, kamikazes and shore batteries, in addition to surviving the storms at sea and evacuating the prisoners of war from Japan.

The Hopping was bound for the Navy Shipyard in Charleston, SC, passed the breakwater at Colon, Canal Zone on December 27 and rounded east end of Cuba on December 29. But they weren't home yet. On December 31 they ran into a storm while crossing the Gulf Stream with wind up to 45 knots and waves 30 feet high. The ship had to slow down and head into storm for several hours before resuming course and speed and arriving Charleston Harbor at 1737 hours.

They were finally at their destination and a relieved footnote was added to the WAR DIARY:

"31 December 1945, 1200 hrs L 31-35N 79-18W.   And so the year ends."

Captain McNulty shared with me that one of his proudest experiences came when he sailed the Hopping alone, independent of any other ships or commanders, from Tokyo, Japan to Charleston, SC. I believed this must have confirmed to him his ability and worthiness as a ship's commander to safely command his ship and crew across the entire stretch of the Pacific Ocean. According to every man I talked with who served on the Hopping during his command vouched that he indeed was a most capable naval commander, highly respected, deeply trusted and always a gentleman.

The USS HOPPING, APD 51 started the month of January, 1946 in the Charleston, SC area. Ammunition was unloaded and the ship put into the Charleston Shipyard for a pre-inactivation overhaul, which continued for the rest of the month. On January 23 the Hopping was notified by message that the ship was to remain in the active fleet and report to Norfolk, VA on February 9. The shipyard which had done very little work up to that point, turned to and did their best in the one week's availability remaining. Demobilization had taken its toll of men but some experienced petty officers were obtained when the ship was put back into the active fleet. The Hopping completed its overhaul on February 1 and the next day reported for duty with Task Division 21.

It was noted that during the ship's stay in the yard one bent frame was sustained and the starboard depth charge racks were bent out of shape twice due to the strong ebb tide and careless ship handling by the yard tugs. All three times the Hopping was moored.

On February 18, the Hopping left Charleston sailing independently for Norfolk arriving on February 19. On February 28 the USS WILLIAM T. POWELL, DE 213, dragged anchor and collided with the Hopping denting the Hopping's bow and punching a small hole in the starboard truck compartment. Repairs were made. Men and officers were separated as their time came due but most replacements were made. On March 21 the Hopping received orders to proceed back to Charleston shipyard for pre-inactivation overhaul and on March 22 sailed with the USS SIMS, APD 50 to Charleston. The Hopping and Sims had been together throughout the Atlantic and Pacific service. The pre-inactivation overhaul was completed and on April 26, 1946 the Hopping sailed from Charleston to Green Cove Springs, FL where it was assigned to the 16th Fleet and was deactivated.

On April 30, 1946 Captain Willard J. McNulty signed the last submission of the ship's WAR DIARY. The Hopping received one battle star for service at the Battle of Okinawa.

The officers and men who served on her had witnessed the harsh, cold dangers of the North Atlantic Ocean and the fiercest battles ever waged in the history of mankind in the Pacific Ocean. All but two returned home, some in better shape than others, thanks to the dedication and skill of the officers and men who fulfilled their duty and responsibility to each other and to their country.

The USS HOPPING, DE 155/APD 51, had proven to be a worthy warship in all kinds of situations and peril and performed an outstanding service to her officers and men and for her country. She was decommissioned May 5, 1947 when she entered the Atlantic Reserve Fleet and remained berth until she was struck from the Navy List in September, 1964. She was sold on August 15, 1966 to Boston Metals Co., Baltimore, MD.

"The DE legacy is a story of an astonishingly able, mass-produced vessel that made a critical difference in the successful war at sea in World War II. Importantly, it is the story of the Navy and Coast Guard men who served in these ships, men heroic in combat, long-suffering in endless watches, capable of enduring cruel seas, cold, heat, boredom, waiting, watching, then suddenly rising to amazing capability in crisis.

                    Rear Admiral Sheldon Kinney
                    U. S. Navy, Retired"

(Taken from: Volume 1, Number 1
                1944 Destroyer Escort Historical Foundation
                Published by The Destroyer Escort Sailors Association
                for The Destroyer Escort Historical Foundation)

USS HOPPING DE 155/APD 51
PORT OF CALL

May 27, 1943	Commissioned USS HOPPING DE 155, Portsmouth, Va.	
June 12, 1943	Departed Norfolk, Va	
June 16, 1943	Arrived Bermuda Island	Departed July 10, 1943
July 12, 1943	Arrived Norfolk, Va	Departed August 15, 1943
Sept. 2, 1943	Arrived Casablanca, Morocco	Departed Sept. 6, 1943
Sept. 7, a943	Arrived Gilbraltar, Spain	Departed Sept. 8, 1943
Sept. 25, 1943	Arrived Brooklyn, NY	Departed October 11, 1943
October 24, 1943	Arrived Londonderry, Northern Ireland	Departed October 30, 1943
Nov. 9, 1943	Arrived Brooklyn, NY	Departed Nov. 19, 1943
Nov. 20, 1943	Arrived CascoBay, Maine	Departed Nov. 29, 1943
Nov. 30, 1943	Arrived Brooklyn, NY	Departed Dec. 2, 1943
Dec. 12, 1943	Arrived Londonderry, Northern Ireland	Departed Dec. 19,1943
January 5, 1944	Arrived Brooklyn, NY	Departed January 19,1944
January 30, 1944	Arrived Londonderry, Northern Ireland	Departed Feb. 7, 1944
Feb. 17, 1944	Arrived Brooklyn, NY	Departed Feb. 29, 1944
March 1, 1944	Arrived Casco Bay, Maine	Departed March 6, 1944
March 7, 1944	Arrived Staten Island, NY	Departed March 10, 1944
March 20, 1944	Arrived Lisahally, Northern Ireland	Departed March 27, 1944
April 6, 1944	Arrived Brooklyn, NY	Departed April 24, 1944
May 7, 1944	Arrived Londonderry, Northern Ireland	Departed May 10, 1944
May 20, 1944	Arrived Brooklyn, NY	Departed June 8, 1944
June 20, 1944	Arrived Lisahally, Northern Ireland	Departed June 24, 1944
July 4, 1944	Arrived Brooklyn, NY	Departed July 18, 1944
July 29, 1944	Arrived Lisahally, Northern Ireland	Departed August 4, 1944
August 14, 1944	Arrived Bayone, NJ	Departed August 23, 1944
August 25, 1944	Arrived Brooklyn, NY	Departed August 27, 1944
Sept. 9, 1944	Arrived Portsmouth, England	Departed Sept. 10, 1944
Sept. 10, 1944	Arrived Cherbourg, France	Departed Sept. 12, 1944
Sept. 23, 1944	Arrived Staten Island, NY	

USS HOPPING DE 155 converted to APD 51

Dec. 1, 1944	Departed Staten Island, NY	
Dec. 2, 1944	Arrived Norfolk, Va	Departed Dec. 20, 1944
Dec. 25, 1944	Arrived Cristobal, Panama Canal Zone	Departed Dec. 26, 1944
January 3, 1945	Arrived San Diego, CA	Departed January 9, 1945
January 15, 1945	Arrived Pearl Harbor, Terr. of Hawaii	Departed January 17, 1945
January 17, 1945	Arrived Maui, Terr. of Hawaii	Departed February 8, 1945

	February 18, 1945 Crossed the International Date Line	
Feb. 22, 1945	Arrived Eniwetok, Marshall Islands	Departed Feb. 23, 1945
March 4, 1945	Arrived Leyte, Philippine Islands	Departed March 21. 1945
March 26, 1945	Arrived Kerama Retto, Ryukyu Islands	Departed March 27, 1945
March 27, 1945	Arrived Okinawa	Departed April 10, 1945
April 10, 1945	Arrived Kerama Retto, Ryukyu Islands	Departed April 14, 1945
April 23, 1945	Arrived Ulithi, Caroline Islands	Departed May 11, 1945
May 17, 1945	Arrived Okinawa	Departed July 8, 1945
July 8, 1945	Arrived Kume Shima, Ryukyu Islands	Departed July 13, 1945
July 13, 1945	Arrived Okinawa	Departed August 8, 1945
August 11, 1945	Arrived Samar, Philippine Islands	Departed August 20, 1945
August 23, 1945	Arrived Okinawa	Departed Sept. 9, 1945
Sept. 11, 1945	Arrived Wakayama, Japan	Departed Sept. 15, 1945
Sept. 19, 1945	Guam, Mariana Islands	Departed Sept. 21, 1945
Sept. 25, 1945	Wakayama, Japan	Departed October 1, 1945
October 2, 1945	Yokahama, Japan	Departed October 12, 1945
October 17, 1945	San Pedro, Philippine Islands	Departed October 18, 1945
October 18, 1945	Guiana Samar, Philippine Islands	Departed October 20, 1945
October 29, 1945	San Pedro Bay, Philippine Islands	Departed October 27, 1945
October 29, 1945	Manila, Philippine Islands	Departed Nov. 2, 1945
Nov. 2, 1945	Subic Bay, Philippine Islands	Departed Nov. 2, 1945
Nov. 14, 1945	Yokahama, Japan	Departed Nov. 16, 1945
Nov. 16, 1945	Yokosuka, Japan	Departed Nov. 24, 1945
	Home Bound Banner Flying	
	November 29, 1945 Crossed the International Date Line	
Nov. 29, 1945	Midway Island	Departed Nov. 30, 1945
Dec. 4, 1945	Pearl Harbor, Terr. of Hawaii	Departed Dec. 5, 1945
Dec. 11, 1945	San Diego, CA	Departed Dec. 17, 1945
Dec. 26, 1945	Panama Canal Zone	Departed Dec. 27, 1945
Dec. 31, 1945	Charleston, SC	Departed Feb. 16, 1946
Feb. 19, 1946	Norfolk, VA	Departed March 22, 1946
March 23, 1946	Charleston, SC	Departed April 26, 1946
April 27, 1946	Green Cove Springs, FL	

The USS HOPPING DE 155/APD 51 was decommissioned on May 5, 1947
Struck from the US Navy List in September 1964
Sold to Boston Metals Company, Baltimore, MD on August 15, 1966

FINIS

Chapter 13

Dad's Homecoming, Successes and Trials

Dad arrived in San Francisco in mid-August, 1945 on board the USS HAMUL, AD 20 and was transferred to the U. S. Fleet Hospital No. 103 located on Treasure Island. On August 18 he was presented the PURPLE HEART MEDAL "for wounds received in action against an enemy of the United States on April 9, 1945" by Lt. Cmd. T. E. Hammond for Captain E. F. Helmkamp, C. O.

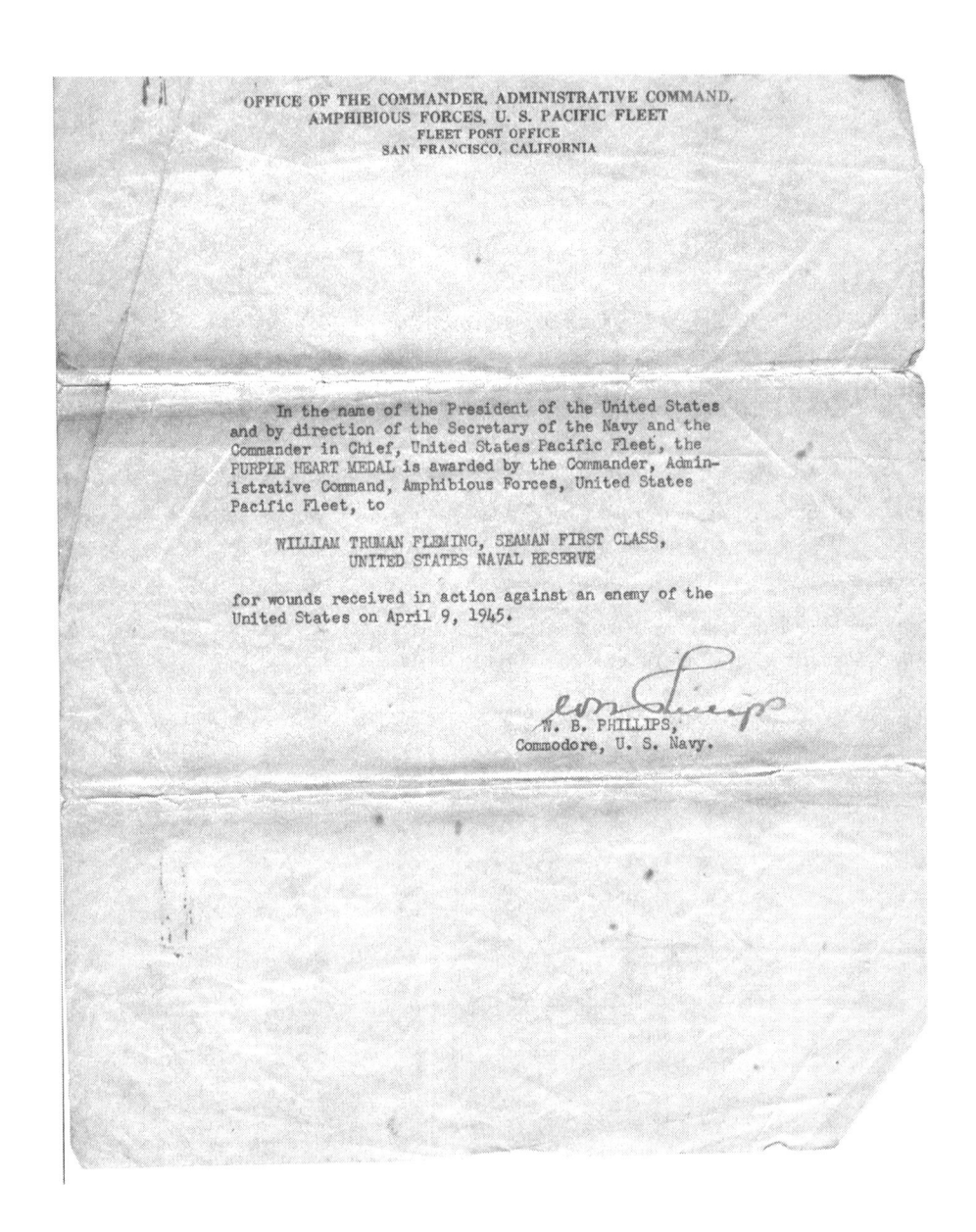

> OFFICE OF THE COMMANDER, ADMINISTRATIVE COMMAND,
> AMPHIBIOUS FORCES, U. S. PACIFIC FLEET
> FLEET POST OFFICE
> SAN FRANCISCO, CALIFORNIA
>
> In the name of the President of the United States and by direction of the Secretary of the Navy and the Commander in Chief, United States Pacific Fleet, the PURPLE HEART MEDAL is awarded by the Commander, Administrative Command, Amphibious Forces, United States Pacific Fleet, to
>
> WILLIAM TRUMAN FLEMING, SEAMAN FIRST CLASS,
> UNITED STATES NAVAL RESERVE
>
> for wounds received in action against an enemy of the United States on April 9, 1945.
>
> W. B. PHILLIPS,
> Commodore, U. S. Navy.

On the same date he also received an Honorable Discharge from the United States Navy along with the monthly rate of pay of $66.00 and furnished with a travel allowance of five cents per mile from San Francisco to Clintwood, Virginia and was paid in full the total amount of $166.85. He rode the train to Abingdon, Virginia where he was picked up by a family member.

Neither my brothers nor I remember when he arrived home but we all clearly remember he was frail and had lost a considerable amount of weight. He remained at home for quite a while unable to work or travel any distance because he was in considerable pain from a back injury. It became apparent that his injury at Okinawa was definitely a severe wound to his back and he confided to the family that when the ship was hit the concussion blast hit his back and knocked him over the body of a man as he ran to his battle station leaving small pieces of shrapnel in his back and buttock. The ship's casualty report, however, states that he only received fragment wounds to his left hand. The back injury probably accounts for the several transfers he had from the Hopping to other ships "for treatment" and back to the Hopping before he was finally transferred on July 25 to the Hamul bound for San Francisco.

I have a government form that Dad made an application for readjustment of veteran benefits and his application was rejected on October 25, 1945 because his official discharge states, "Honorable Discharge – Is physically qualified for discharge." It is possible the Hopping's medical officer did not correct the original casualty report and, therefore, just the hand wound remained on his record.

In my reading about the men who returned from World War II it came to light several times that these men were so anxious to get home and to get on with their lives that many did not reveal their injuries especially if they were not noticeable. It is apparent to the family that this was Dad's situation. He suffered greatly from the back wound and was diagnosed in the Veterans Hospital and by local doctors that he had severe kidney wounds. I personally have been with him on several occasions when he passed blood and even small pieces of kidney through his urinary tract. During these "spells" he would become very rigid throughout his body, perspire profusely and cry out in pain. At one point in 1948 he became addicted to morphine which was given to him by a local doctor to ease the pain. Mother interceded by denying the morphine to him when he was confined to his bed for several days. 1945 was before a kidney transplant was common; therefore, he simply had to live with the injury until it took his life. During this time the Veteran's Hospital in Johnson City, TN offered to treat him as best they could but he refused to stay in hospital for any length of time.

He remained at home from September, 1945 until the spring of 1946 before he regained enough strength to do light work. During this time he would do a lot of the cooking and baking for the family. My brothers and I remember this well because it was the first time we had experienced home made bread with yeast and donuts. In fact, when he was transferred to the Hamul on April 24 for treatment of wounds he states in the Diary, "Will go on watch tomorrow morning with bakers." Therefore his duty must have been as a baker on this ship.

Included in the pocket sized Diary are recipes, i.e., "Doughnuts, Fried, 600 rations: Sugar-6 lbs; Shortening-12 ozs; Salt-3 ozs; Eggs, Fresh-3 doz; Flour 18 lbs; Bk. Powder-12 ozs; Pwd. Milk-2 qts; Nutmeg-4 ozs; For basic sweet dough use 12 ozs. Yeast & 3 lbs. Sugar; No Bk. Pwd." There are other recipes for "Navy Chocolate Icing", "Light Marshmallows", "Corn Bread, 4 sheet pans", "Apple Fillings", "Plain Cake, 4 sheet pans", "Pie Crust, 4 pans", "Frosting", Pumpkin Pie", "Chocolate Cake", "Cream Icing", "Oatmeal Cookies, 300-400 rations", "Sweet Rolls, 18 - 2 lb. Loaves", "Baking Pwd. Biscuits, 300-350 rations", "Cinnamon Buns, 300-400 rations", "Cream Pie Filling, 18 - 10 in. pies", "Custard Pie Filling", "Yellow Cake" and "Ginger Cookies", all with similar size ingredients. Looks to me like the sailors ate well from the bakery.

In 1946 the US military began downsizing by selling surplus vehicles and equipment. Dad saw the opportunity to purchase the large army trucks for hauling coal. He and Mother went to Richmond, VA and Norfolk, VA several times and purchased these trucks to start a trucking business. My brothers and I remember them returning from these trips with Mother driving one of the trucks loaded with the 1941 Ford car they had purchased and Dad driving another truck loaded with a jeep or 3/4 ton ammunition carrier.

The same year he opened a small grocery store and we delivered groceries to neighbors in the 3/4 ton truck. He began in the latter part of 1946 driving one of the coal trucks and managed to continue doing this for about a year although he suffered with back pain. In the meantime mother operated the grocery store.

They were entrepreneurs and always looking for business opportunities. One day Dad purchased 1500 seeding trees to be planted on a piece of the farm that was unproductive and could be harvested in a few years for a nice profit. So he sent Charles, Bill and me to plant them. We planted about 150 before we started wrestling and playing until late in the day. Then we took the remaining seedlings and planted all of them in a big stump on the back side of the property. When Dad came home that day he asked how we did with the planting and we informed him that we planted all of them, which we did. He said he doubted that and would check later. Fortunately for us he never check because if he had discovered what we really did the belt or razor strap would have found our backsides and we would have been sent to complete the job.

In 1947 he decided to campaign for the office of Sheriff of Dickenson County. Since we were a strong family unit the entire family became active in the campaign, especially my older brothers and I. I remember knocking on doors to distribute flyers, campaign literature and asking people to vote for my Dad. I followed the election process closely and was in the court house the evening the results were announced. Dad won by the largest margin any county official had ever had to that point. In addition, a very good friend of Dad's was elected the same time by the name of Barnum Powers. He was a brother to Darrell "Shifty" Powers in the book **The Band of Brothers**.

He took office in January, 1948 and the family moved to the apartment adjoining the county jail and court house in Clintwood. As sheriff, Dad also was the jailer. I recall some exciting times while we lived there. On one occasion a woman was arrested for public drunkenness and hanged herself with her belt but she was discovered and cut down before she died. On another, I was just arriving home from basketball practice when a prisoner was escaping from Dad and a deputy. I dropped my books and ran to the office. When Dad saw me he told me to go get him. I ran him down in about 100 yards and held him until Dad arrived. The man just laughed and said to Dad, "I would have made it if this young fellow hadn't caught me." Dad quietly handcuffed him and we led him back to his cell. There was a man well known throughout the community for his outstanding guitar playing and Saturday night public drunkenness. He was a regular visitor to the jail and when he sobered up Dad would give him his guitar in his cell. He would play for hours at a time and I would join him on the opposite bunk. He was really harmless and I enjoyed his music. Several times Dad allowed prisoners to take one of his personal trucks and go do jobs in the community. On one of the "outings" the driver who was a handsome young man charged with a

Vote For

Truman Fleming
Candidate For
SHERIFF
Election Nov. 4, 1947

relatively minor offense decided to leave. The other five or six prisoners refused to go with him and even called the jail and asked someone to come get them. I went and drove the truck and prisoners back to the jail. Dad wasn't concerned about the "escapee" and simply said, "He'll be back." Sure enough, three days later he showed up looking haggled, with a three day beard and informed Dad he just had to go see his girlfriend. Dad took him to his cell and nothing was ever mentioned about his "escape" again and no additional charges were placed. I even had the experience of going to break up a moonshine still with he and his deputies. We loaded into two trucks and a car. Dad drove one of the trucks and I rode with him. He drove to the gate of the farm and all three vehicles were driven about a quarter mile to the still. It was a large operation with lots of brew cooking. Dad told the deputies to proceed cutting up the copper and destroying the still and load everything on the trucks and that no one would get hurt. He pointed to three men looking at us from the brow of the hill. He knew the owner and had sent word ahead of us that we were coming to capture the still and he didn't want any trouble. When the job was completed we returned to the jail and unloaded it for county pickup. On another occasion Dad sent me with 42 gallons of moonshine to pour down the town storm drain. He kept one gallon for evidence because the person responsible had been arrested for possession of illegal alcohol and had a court date set. There was a room in the jail where all evidence for court was kept and in it was illegal alcohol, weapons of all kinds and other evidence, yet, our doors were never locked and we never had a concern about an intruder.

An extraordinary event happened early in his administration when one of his deputies was killed by a man who held a grudge against the deputy for having him arrested for military desertion. Dad and other deputies solved the case and arrested the killer. This story made national news and was published in a national magazine. I have a copy of the entire article but there are no identifications of the name of the magazine or dates. On the following page is a picture of the title page of the article.

By these few examples one can gather that Dad engendered trust with other people. He was known for his fair and equal treatment and gave respect to all people.

Brother Charles joined the navy in 1948 and after boot camp at Great Lakes was assigned duty on the USS NEWPORT NEWS, a large cruiser, where he served until 1952 and brother Bill purchased a motor cycle and went to work. I enjoyed the challenges school offered and the team sports I participated in throughout high school and on into college. In fact, I played on the high school basketball teams from 1949 -1953 that still holds the Virginia High School League record for the most consecutive wins - 66.

During the period of 1948 through 1950 Dad had periods of illness due to the kidney wound and was confined to the hospital or home for several days at a time. In late 1950 an opening came at the state level for the regional Alcoholic Beverage Control Agent for our area and he resigned the office of sheriff and took that job. In 1952 another blessing was added to the family when our youngest sister, Margaret Charlene, was born. Mother was 40 and Dad was 39. In 1953 I graduated from high school and went off to college. From this time on Dad's health began to deteriorate and so did the relationship between Mother and him until she took the three girls and moved to Alexandria, VA. In 1957, I

case of the COCKY KILLER

He took active part in the manhunt. He believed that he was too smart to get caught!

Following his confession, the killer (hatless) led the hounds and their owners (left) and Sheriff Truman Fleming and Deputies Ross Phillips and Delman Rosnick over getaway trail.

finished college and volunteered for the Army. During the time of April to November, 1957 I was called home on emergency leave at least five times because Dad was in the hospital in critical condition. In November, 1957 I was transferred to Germany and in March, 1958 I was called home due to his critical health. I arrived at the hospital to find Mother and Brother Charles at his bedside. Mother asked him if he recognized me and he acknowledged he did. Just before this he asked Mother to forgive him for the pain he had caused her and said he was prepared to meet his Savior. Within one hour after that he died in our presence on April 2, 1958. The immediate cause of death was Uremia which is an accumulation in the blood of material normally passed off in the urine resulting in a poisoned condition. This condition was caused by Chronic Pyelonephritis which is an inflamation of the renal pelvis located in or near the kidneys. In layman's term, his kidneys stopped functioning.

Dad's long and painful journey from the Battle of Okinawa when he was wounded on April 9, 1945 was over. He suffered greatly and so did Mother and the family. Even though the war had ended nearly thirteen years before the result of the war had finally ended for Dad and his family.

Within a year after his death his mother, our grandmother, died and, as usual, Mother made another bold move. With very little money and lots of faith she bought the farm where she and Dad had started their lives together in 1930. She began work, literally with a pick and shovel in hand, and in less than five years had developed a portion of the farm into a profitable business venture and within five more years was living somewhat comfortably. Her business grew and she made investments that also grew so that the last 20 - 25 years of her life she lived productively and prosperously. She continued to manage her business, investments and personal finances until her death on November 14, 1999 at the age of 88 years.

Mother with her seven children and their spouses
Tanglewood Resort, NC, April, 1999

Chapter 14

Friends And War Heroes

Everyone who served our country during this great war is admired for his bravery, achievements and qualities. Each person's story, if told, would be fascinating and laudable. Yet, they were not seeking fame or recognition. They were only accepting their responsibility to contribute to the preservation of the American way of life and to the freedom from oppression of other people around the world. They were and are true heroes and more people should follow their example. Not only did they achieve victory but as they returned to their homes and communities they contributed to possibly the greatest social, industrial and economical advancements in the history of mankind.

It has been my privilege to have met and associated with some of the men who served on the USS HOPPING, DE 155/APD 51. They have always welcomed me and my wife into their reunions with open arms and loving hearts. My only regret is that I did not pursue earlier acquaintance in order to have met more of those who served along side my dad. They all have my deepest admiration and respect.

The following pictures are an effort to recognize a few of the ones I have come to know over the past four years at their reunions.

Fred and Mozella Wallenfelsz, Branson, MO Reunion 2002

Fred Wallenfelsz is the cousin Dad mentioned on April 8, 1944 when he first boarded the Hopping. He was also the first member of the Hopping crew I met at my first reunion in 2001. After Dad was elected sheriff, Fred came to Clintwood and Dad assisted him in getting a job in the coal industry and then encouraged him to take advantage of the GI Bill. He wrote a letter of recommendation and helped him get

Robert M. "Shorty" Miller, Darrell Fleming, Al Caiafa, Fred Wallensfelzs, September 23, 2001, Orlando, FL.

accepted at Milligan College where he graduated with a degree in education and became a teacher. Later he left education and owned and operated a successful business in Front Royal, VA where he and Mozella now reside.

Shorty Miller boarded the Hopping when it was commissioned on May 21, 1943 and left January 17, 1946. He was awarded the Bronze Star Medal for his outstanding service during the crisis when the Hopping was hit on April 9, 1945. He has been an invaluable resource to me throughout the five years of research. He now lives in Phoenix, AZ. Al Caiafa boarded the Hopping February 21, 1944 and left April 7, 1946. When I first met Al he said he knew Dad well because he probably saved his life when Dad fell across him when the ship was hit at Okinawa. Al is, more than likely, the wounded man Dad said he remembered falling across as he ran to his battle station. Al lives in Chicago, IL. Fred Wallenfelzs boarded the Hopping February 21, 1944 and left February 15, 1946. He and Al Caiafa have remained in close contact since their days on the Hopping.

*Darrell Fleming, Captain Willard Jerald McNulty, Kathy Fleming
September 23, 2001, Orlando FL.*

Captain McNulty boarded the Hopping January 9, 1944 as the Executive Officer, promoted to Commander of the ship on August 16, 1944 and left April 30, 1946 when the ship was officially deactivated. He lived the latter part of his life in Kingsville, TX and died on March 28, 2004. His eldest daughter, Patricia Brenn, MD, in a letter presented a brief tribute of her father, "As you know, he was respected and well loved by his friends and by his community of Kingsville and the various organizations in which he was active..........I feel fortunate that I was able to know my father better in the last few years. He was a modest and kind man of high intelligence and a generous man, giving freely of his service to the community until December 2003."

To a man who served under his command and with whom I spoke had high praise and sincere respect for his leadership aboard the Hopping and considered him a dear friend as he joined in their many reunions. His presence will be deeply missed by all who knew him.

John "Jack" Fleming and Darrell Fleming September 23, 2001

Jack Fleming boarded the Hopping on May 21, 1943 when it was commissioned and left in July, 1944 to attend school and was assigned to another destroyer. He did not know Dad as they were assigned to different stations. As far as we know they were not kinsmen. Jack lives in West Roxbury, MA.

*The Hopping Reunion, September, 2001, Orlando, FL
Thirteen Shipmates with Spouses and Friends*

*Lyle Buchanan and Darrell Fleming at Orlando Reunion
September 23, 2001*

Lyle and Marie Buchanan, Ralph "Bud" Barnes and Friends and Al and Pat Vilardi at the Orlando Reunion, September 22, 2001

Lyle Buchanan boarded the Hopping on July 5, 1944 and left on September 20, 1945. He died February 28, 2005. Ralph "Bud" Barnes boarded the Hopping when it was commissioned on May 21, 1943 and left on August 30, 1945. He died on January 15, 2005.

Yolanda Caiafa, Dick and Wilma Smith and Sal Trio Branson, MO Reunion September, 2002

Yolanda Caiafa is the wife of Al Caiafa. Dick Smith boarded the Hopping, February 21, 1944 and left April 3, 1946. Dick returned to civilian life and developed a family of several car dealerships in Columbia, SC. Sal Trio boarded the Hopping May 21, 1943 when it was commissioned and left March 15, 1946. He lives in West Caldwell, NJ.

Ensign Edward H. Cundiff boarded the Hopping in late 1944 and left February 13, 1946. Ed graduated from Duke University. He and Betty live in St. Louis, MO. Ed and Bill Wenzel have remained close friends.

Ed and Betty Cundiff, Branson, MO Reunion September 2002

Robert "Bob" Tero boarded the Hopping February 21, 1944 and left May 8, 1946. He lives in Whitman MA. Even though Bob has a physical impairment from a stroke, he eagerly attends all reunions. He was the seaman standing by the rail in the picture of the burial at sea.

Bob Tero, Branson, MO Reunion, September 2002

*Willis "Bill" and Barbara Dailey,
Branson Reunion, September 22, 2002*

Bill Dailey boarded the Hopping June 5, 1943 and left January 10, 1946. He and Barbara live in Oneonta, NY. Bill was in communications aboard the Hopping and shared letters he wrote to his family regarding his observations of the torpedoeing of the USS DONNELL, DE 56.

*Frank and Connie Jones with Dick Smith and Bill Dailey in background,
Branson Reunion, September 22, 2002*

Frank Jones boarded the Hopping May 21, 1943, when it was commissioned and left March 19, 1945. Frank lives in Newberry Park, CA.

*The Hopping Reunion, September 21, 2002, Branson, MO.
Shipmates, spouses and friends with Jim Stafford of The Jim Stafford Show.*

*Pigeon Forge, TN Reunion, September 17, 2003
Rob Davidson, survivor of the Donnell, visiting
with the Hopping shipmates after 59 years*

Reunion, Pigeon Forge, TN, September 17, 2003
Front Row: Darrell Fleming, Jack Fleming, Bud Barnes, Bob Tero, Frank Jones, Fred Wallenfelzs, Sal Trio, Dick Smith, Dick Owen
Back Row: Richard Smith, Al Viliardi, Shorty Miller, Al Caiafa

Dick and Wilma Smith with son, Richard
Reunion Cruise, November 12, 2004 in conjunction with the USS REEVES and the USS DONNELL

Charles, my brother, and wife Amilee Fleming, making a presentation to Al Caiafa at the Pigeon Forge, TN Reunion, September 17, 2003

Al and Pat Vilardi with Dick and Wilma Smith, Reunion Cruise, November 12, 2004 with the USS REEVES and USS DONNELL

Al Vilardi boarded the Hopping October 11, 1945 and left March 6, 1946. Al, with a lot of help from Pat, has been the coordinator of the reunions for the last five years and has always done an outstanding job. Al and Pat live in Sebastian, FL

The number of remaining shipmates is growing thin with the passing of each year and those who are able to attend are few. It will be a sad day for them when they can no longer attend and enjoy the fellowship that began over 60 years ago when they were ever so young with big dreams and a willing heart to serve their country at a time of great need. As long as they live the memory of their time on the USS HOPPING, DE 155/APD 51 and their fellow shipmates will remain. Let those of us who follow never forget what they did for us.

TAPS

Day is done, gone the sun
From the lakes, from the hills, from the sky
All is well, safely rest, God is nigh.

Fading light, dims the sight
And a star, gems the sky, gleaming bright
From afar, drawing nigh, falls the night.

Thanks and praise, for our days
Neath the sun, neath the stars, neath the sky
As we go, this we know, God is nigh.